THE CROSSING OF THE VISIBLE

Cultural Memory in the Present

Mieke Bal and Hent de Vries, Editors

THE CROSSING OF THE VISIBLE

Jean-Luc Marion

Translated by James K. A. Smith

STANFORD UNIVERSITY PRESS

STANFORD, CALIFORNIA

2004

Stanford University Press
Stanford, California

The Crossing of the Visible was originally published in French in 1996 under the title *La Croisée du visible*,

This book has been published with the assistance of the French Ministry of Culture—National Center for the Book.

Printed in the United States of America
on acid-free, archival-quality paper

Library of Congress Cataloging-in-Publication Data

Marion, Jean-Luc, 1946–
[Croisee du visible. English]
The crossing of the visible / Jean-Luc Marion ;
translated by James K. A. Smith.
p. cm. — (Cultural memory in the present)
ISBN 0-8047-3391-0 (cloth : alk. paper) —
ISBN 0-8047-3392-9 (pbk. : alk. paper)
1. Visual perception. 2. Perspective. 3. Painting—Philosophy. 4. Phenomenology. I. Title. II. Series.
ND1140.M3513 2004
750'.1'8—DC22

2003021461

Typeset by Tim Roberts in 11/13.5 Adobe Garamond

Original Printing 2004

Contents

Preface

The question of painting does not pertain first or only to painters, much less only to aestheticians. It concerns visibility itself, and thus pertains to everything—to sensation in general.

In truth, one is restricted to what one can see and where one can go. And this is certainly why philosophy cannot refrain from finding itself, when it comes to painting, permanently. This is because philosophy today has become, essentially, phenomenology; yet phenomenology no longer pretends to return to the things themselves, because it has undertaken the task of seeing what gives itself [*ce qui se donne*]—what gives [*ce que cela donne*]. The exceptional visibility of the painting has thus become a privileged case of the phenomenon, and therefore one possible route to a consideration of phenomenality in general.

But is it enough for phenomenology to delimit visibility and thus every possible painting [*tableaux*]? Does not the painting admit itself only to a singular status rather than to a merely domestic collection of general possibilities? In the movement from the idol to the icon, we of course follow early research, but we follow above all the necessity of the thing itself: the painting—the visible par excellence—offers a dilemma of two figures of appearance, inverted, opposed, but nevertheless indispensable and inseparable. Theology becomes, in this situation, an indisputable authority [*instance*] concerning any theory of painting. Having sometimes denied this, other times simply forgotten it, aesthetic thought finds itself entangled in long aporias. Perhaps the time has come for it to deliver itself and to see the visible face-to-face, as a gift of appearance.

The studies collected here were produced in response to invitations. In my eyes, this gives them a special value: without the trust of inviting friends, I would never have been able to develop by myself what I then attempted in expounding them. Thus I am returning today what was first offered to me. But, among all those who urged me to think and speak where I did not want to venture, among them Michel and Anne Henry, it is to the friendship of Alain Bonfand that I owe the most. He is to be truly thanked here. As for the insufficiencies of my project, one could attribute them to the traditional vanity of philosophy, which always says more than it knows—but often less than it thinks.

Lods, December, 1990

THE CROSSING OF THE VISIBLE

1

The Crossing of the Visible and the Invisible

I

In itself, perspective[1] exercises a paradox. Even more than that, perspective and paradox are determined by similar characters: both indicate the visible entirely in its withdrawing, discretely but radically. The paradox attests to the visible, while at the same time opposing itself, or rather, while inverting itself; literally, it constitutes a counter-visible, a counter-seen, a counter-appearance that offers in a spectacle[2] to be seen the opposite of what, at first sight, one would expect to see. More than a surprising opinion, the paradox often points to a miracle—it makes visible that which one should not be able to see and which one is not able to see without astonishment [*stupeur*]. Thus, in the Septuagint, the works of God in liberating Israel from Egypt themselves produce paradoxes, known as miracles: "See what is most paradoxical [παραδόξότατον]: in water that extinguishes, the fire increases its power" (Wisdom 16:17). In this sense, or rather, in another sense that will soon become precisely the inverse of this, the human face offers a paradox to be seen; in the words of Char: "As the bee leaves the orchard for the fruit already black, so the women supported without betraying the paradox of this face that did not have characteristics of a hostage."[3] A paradox of the face, which finds itself fulfilled in this "strange paradox in Christ (πάραδοξον), the Lord in the form of a servant, the divine glory (δόξα) within the strictures of the human."[4] The paradox testifies here that what enters into visibility is that which one should not have encountered there: fire in water, divinity in humanity; the paradox is born from the intervention of the invisible in the visible, whatever it might be. From this arises the necessary effect of the paradox, in thought but also in the sensible: it dazzles, taking the mind by surprise and shocking the gaze [*la vue*][5] in such a way that, far from fulfilling or satiating[6] them, its very excess of visibility injures them. Just as the miracles give rise to so much resistance that their reality cannot be questioned, so theoretical paradoxes stimulate polemic much more than they stimulate the production of evidence. —And yet perspective, in its own way, also provokes a paradox. Or rather, it imitates the paradox, by inverting the relation it has established between the visible and the invisible. In the two operations, the gaze strives to see what it is not able to see, but differently: the paradox offers a counter-appearance, while perspective suggests a breakthrough of the gaze. The paradox poses a visible that belies the visible, perspective a gaze that pierces through the visible. Moreover, in classical Latin, *perspicuus* qualifies what offers itself as transparent to the gaze, for example a vestment; and in fact, in perspective, the gaze pierces through what one would call, for lack of a better term, a middle ground [*milieu*], a milieu so transparent that it neither stops nor slows down the gaze but allows it to rush through, without any resistance, as if it were a vacuum [*vide*]. In the case of perspective, the gaze pierces the void [*le vide*],[7] without any obstacle or limit other than its own exhaustion; not only does it cross through this void, since it does not aim at any object defined by a horizon, but perspective's gaze pierces the void without end because it crosses through it for nothing; in perspective, the gaze loses itself in the void—more specifically, it aims at emptiness, outstripping every object once and for all, in order to aim at this void itself. In this, moreover, it loses itself only to find itself there continually.

What void? Here it is not a question of a physical void, which, as a pure absence of things, a real [*réelle*] breakdown of *res*, gives nothing to be seen but rather gives only vertigo. A physical void: there is nothing to be seen, no new spectacle, but conversely, the real void of reality [*le vide réel de la réalité*], as a desert of things, where I then enter, am moved, live, possibly fall and, when it ends, crash upon the final frontier. This desert of things I then almost see, as opposed to other things that mark or signal its boundaries in a way that renders the void visible. The physical void, precisely because it defines itself as a visible desert of things, remains reified, real, visible. On the contrary, the void that opens itself to the gaze in perspective does not open itself as a real "traversable" space that could be inhabited or defined, nor does it add anything to the store of visible things, not even a visible void. The void of perspective does not add anything to the real visible, since it puts it on the scene. In effect, in perspective my gaze invisibly traverses the visible, in such a way that, without undergoing any addition to the real, it becomes that much *more* visible: the auditorium that houses us today would not appear habitable to me, and strictly speaking would not be so, if, while crossing a certain invisible emptiness, my gaze was not rendered vast. For it is my gaze, opened up by perspective, that separates these colored surfaces to be seen and made out as walls, that raises this other clear surface to see there and make out a ceiling, that finally levels out this darker surface in order to recognize the unfolding of a ground where I can put my feet. Better, without the invisible space that separates them, we would not be able to recognize the surfaces in what would remain simply patches of color, amassed without order, or sense, or figure, piled up one on top of the other, without the slightest crack, thus requiring that we be subjected to a test to determine if our eyes are functioning like a kind of camera. In other words, more simply, if my gaze did not have the strange habitual property described as binocular vision, if it thus did not have an ability to deal with space, precisely the strained character of invisible space as the dense and confusing aggregate of the visible, then the auditorium containing us would not appear to us as—therefore would not be—spacious: we would be stifled by the promiscuous lack of differentiation of surfaces, to the extent that we would perceive not even surfaces but rather spots and colored shadows. With the visible coming to crush us, anguish would beset us, just as it did the prisoner who, in Poe's *The Pit and the Pendulum*, saw the walls inexorably closing in upon him. A quotidian Samson, the gaze of perspective separates the visible by the equal power of the invisible, in a way that renders it for us vast, inhabitable, organized. Perspective's gaze bores through the visible in order to establish there the invisible distance that renders it aimed-at [*visable*] and first, simply, visible. The gaze instills the invisible in the visible, not indeed to render it less visible but, on the contrary, to render it *more* visible: instead of experiencing chaotically informed impressions, we see there the very visibility of things. Therefore it is the invisible, and it alone, that renders the visible real. Perspective should therefore be first understood not as a historically situated pictorial theory (although it is that also) but as a fundamental role of the gaze, without which we would never see a world. Our gaze reaches a world—exercises its being-in-the-world—because perspective, in the sense of the invisible organizing the visible, has in itself the ability to see through the visible, therefore in terms of the invisible.

The invisible thus released—that is to say, the invisible that releases the visible from itself—radically distinguishes itself from every real void, pure defect, and desert of things. Things fill a real space, which never really empties the conditions of real [*effective*] experience. The real space, empty or not, nevertheless cannot see itself without a gaze. Yet this gaze stretches the visible by the power of the invisible. This operation of perspective, which simply opens up the space of things as a world, is accomplished in a way that depends upon the ideality of space: an ideal space, more real [*effectif*] than real [*réel*], since it is the condition of possibility. The ideality of space itself attests to the experience of dislocation or movement [*déplacement*]: in whatever place I actually find myself located, a thing among things, I organize—indeed, I open—the space between right and left. Kant has definitively established that the perfect similitude of figures, even geometrical ones, is not enough for their superimposition, if it opposes, precisely, the symmetry of difference. Depth would not be able to offer here a recourse, since it also attests to its own ideality: thus, my own face will never be able to become visible to me by a mirror, which always inverts itself according to the tension between right and left. Above all, depth offers the confirmation of what indicates the notions of right and left: whatever my travels might be, depth will always remain in front of me as that which I will never be able to traverse, since, if I advance myself toward and in it, it will deepen itself that much more, so that I am never really able to cover it. The opening of depth always precedes me, since every real advance imitates an ideal advance, forever impassable. In the same way, the difference between right and left can be neither reversed nor abolished, since, in order to be reversed, it would have to be already affirmed. These three dimensions are not themselves measured but rather make possible every measurement of real space: thus they prove their ideality. The irreal [*irréel*],[8] that they organize, must also be described as ideal, and thus also as phenomenological. The two terms designate the same authority: that which makes the visible visible, and which, for the same reason, cannot appear. Perspective becomes an a priori condition of experience and must also be understood in the sense in which Nietzsche speaks of a radical perspectivalism: "As if one could even have a world if one eliminated the perspectivalism!"[9] In other words, as perspectivalism is correlated, for Nietzsche, with interpretation, itself coextensive with the production of phenomena, so perspective, beyond its historical aesthetic meaning, produces the phenomenality of phenomena: by it, the invisible of the gaze is stretched out, arranging and displaying the chaos of the visible as harmonious phenomena.

We are thus better able to conceive how perspective provokes depth [*le relief*], invisibly provokes the visible in its depth [*relief*]. What does depth signify, in effect? Certainly what releases itself, projecting, outside the flat plane, elevating itself and lifting itself up [*relève*].[10] But again, what does this "lifting up" [*relevé*] signify? What is lifted up [*relevé*] is elevated after it has been found to be collapsed, crushed, and damaged. Relief also characterizes—according to the *Littré*—the title for a member of the nobility who, after losing status and land, is taken up by a new family: "Formerly, letters of relief, letters for the rehabilitation of nobility, were properly letters that lifted up [*relèvent*]" (*s.v.* 9). The relief of the visible comes to it from the invisible, which lifts it by deepening and crossing it, to the point of uprooting it from the *humus* of flatness where one encounters only unidimensional perception. The invisible pierces in transparency the visible only in order to raise it, moreover to rehabilitate it, rather than to replace it (as in military "relief") or appease it ("relief" in English). Perspective's gaze ennobles the visible by the invisible and, thus, lifts [*relève*] it up. The invisible gives relief to the visible as one gives a title and a fief [territory]—in order to ennoble. From this the first paradox of perspective must be considered before every painting: the visible increases in direct proportion to the invisible. The more the invisible is increased, the more the visible is deepened.

II

Immediately after being brought back to the painting from some nature outside of the painting, perspective redoubles its paradox. Certainly, at first glance, and in general, the painting limits itself, with the liberty of a brilliance that seems almost unlimited, to the principle that the visible increases in direct proportion to the increase of the invisible. The painting even pushes this paradox to its extreme. For the first visible, the effectively perceived given [*le donné effectivement perçu*], is found to be unquestionably defined here by perfect flatness: a wooden platform, stretched tissue on a frame, part of a wall, the object seen bursts forth to thus speak from a unidimensional poverty; a poor and flat surface, without depth (other than its irregularity and quantity of pigments), or secret, or reserves in which to conceal the least behind-the-scenes [*arrière-spectacle*], and which, nevertheless, deepens itself to a bottomless depth. Consider for example, from the beginning of perspective, historically and narrowly understood, the scenes of the *Legend of the Cross*, in the church of Arezzo, by Piero delle Francesca, nevertheless author (in 1482?) of *On Perspective for Painting*: the levels are there distinguished, between the horse, the soldier, the pikes, and finally the hill where the tent of a peaceful camp is simultaneously being attacked, but the distinction of the levels does not prevent the piling up and even confusion of outlines, the muddling of faces and surfaces. What visible trace is lacking in order to organize this veritable world, in short, to actually create a world? Nothing *visible* is lacking, since all that must appear appears—horse, soldier, banner, tent, and hill—and appears well. If nothing visible is missing, it is thus the invisible that is lacking there.

The situation is quite the reverse, on the other hand, with Raphael's *Marriage of the Virgin*—if one considers it as it ought to be viewed: the main group of characters centers around the hands of the spouses, which are being joined by the priest. But just above them (actually painted within millimeters of their heads) stands a building, whose function is to open itself with a door, then a corridor that gives way, on the other side, through another, similar door, to the sky—a sky framed by the solid heaviness of this building, and disconnected from the real empirical sky, which, moreover, is suspended over every aspect of the scene. The second door opens onto both a strange sky and a real sky; it therefore functions differently from the first; of course, the space that surrounds the first door completes the breakthrough already begun by the lines of the paving stones that extend the balance of the central group. The surfaces are not juxtaposed any more, but rather thrust themselves, from depth into depth [*de profondeur en profondeur*], toward the central opening, which literally inhales them. The entire picture flees toward its vanishing point, the central space, which gives rise to enough space that each surface spreads itself without stifling itself or obfuscating the others. The visible is able to reduce itself since the invisible—the space of the sky encased by the door which is opened onto and by nothing—enables it to be in the open space. The exemplary trait of the placement in perspective in this picture is due not to the imposition of surfaces, which is technically banal, but rather to a paving, a simple sensible transposition of a geometric figure greatly abstracted, so that by the opening through a window that is ultimately unreal, everything visible opens onto the invisible.

This operation can rediscover itself by other means, as in the concave mirror that opens the famous *Portrait of the Betrothal of the Arnolfini* [Van Eyck]. This is certainly a mirror that does not open the painting onto a void [*un vide*], to infinity; but neither does it limit itself to mere circularity, sending it back to itself, in a sterilely closed mimicking of itself. Here the mirror first reveals the reverse (the back) of the two characters that the painting presents face-on, in such a way that we already see more than the first visible, alone real, would allow to be seen. But above all the mirror reveals, beyond the backs of the characters, the faces of three eyewitnesses, who see the couple without directly appearing within the initial painting; this opens itself therefore onto another space that precedes it—a space, moreover, that does not prevent the mirror from reflecting itself in the mirror, thus marking the escape to infinity; therefore it is the invisible that puts it in perspective.[11] Strictly speaking, the invisible thus constructs the visible and allots it.

A similar proportionality of the visible to the depth of perspective, that is to say to the power of the invisible, verifies itself in an infinite number of paintings. We will confine our analysis, arbitrarily, to only one: *Lamentation for Christ*, painted around 1500 by Dürer. The invisible is at work here, less by an actual space that can be located or determined (only the straight corner offers, with an angle of sky, a manner of sensible space) than by the constancy of an oblique rising composition of right and left, repeating itself from surface to surface. On the first level, the body of the dead Christ, an oblique gray extended by a disciple supporting the shoulders of the recumbent effigy. On the second level, three women kneeling alongside the diagonal fixed by Christ. On the third level, the same diagonal repeated by three standing personages and culminating with Saint John, who, from his almost straight head, marks the summit of a pyramid—a conglomeration of nine characters staggered in three parallel diagonals, therefore ordered to the same invisible depth that organizes them without confusion. This pyramid, and even more so the diagonal based upon the Christ, is confirmed by the repetition of many natural pyramids in the lower levels: the hill of Golgotha; an (inevitable) city set on a hill [Matthew 5:14]; finally, two more mountain peaks on the distant horizon again defined by a chain of escarpments. It seems possible to distinguish at least ten different levels, thus ten visible layers. In order that they not be confused, as would be the case if their real juxtaposition were imposed (actually, the spots of colors depend upon and spread themselves all on a unique real surface), it is necessary that there intervene, in a superior number at least of a unity (n + 1), interstices of the invisible. They are only able to rise up, detach, and construct the levels of the visible according to a perfectly irreal supplementary dimension and phenomenological totality. This phenomenological influence of the invisible on the visibly distinguished personages confirms itself *a contrario*: in the foreground, taking center stage, appear the five outlines of the patrons that commissioned the painting; and yet it is a matter of figures on a diminishing scale, disproportionate with the first figure, which they nevertheless precede; their diminished size thus contradicts the organizing principle of perspective, which should have demanded, on the contrary, that they be at least as big as the first body (the corpse of Christ). Elsewhere Van Eyck includes the patrons in the perspective of the painting, on an equal footing with the central religious figure (for example in *The Virgin of Autun*, also known as *The Virgin of Chancellor Rolin*). If Dürer leaves them, on the contrary, in miniature, one must then admit that he excludes them from perspective; the painting is only partially governed by the organizing principle of perspective, which must acknowledge an irreducible margin—the forestage [*l'avant scène*]. Thus perspective clearly acts as a distinct element of the visible, in accordance with a marked boundary that demands it, or better, excludes it; from this it is necessary to conclude that perspective itself is invisible.

The production of the visible by the invisible, even if it testifies to itself first and foremost by perspective narrowly understood, is nevertheless not limited to only this. First because it can make manifest not only the staging of visible levels in depth (as in the Flemish scenes that open themselves from an interior onto a landscape), but more so because it manifests, directly and uniquely, depth itself, in its unreal, almost complete abstraction. Almost complete, for example in Turner's 1804 watercolor *The Pass of Mount St. Gothard*, where every anecdotal detail disappears into an immaterial sky, as though absorbed by the space of the abyssal fault drawn by a sharp trench—a spellbinding depth that inhales the gaze and loses it.[12] Complete abstraction, for example, in the works of Luc Peire, such as his *Environment III*, where an array of straight lines converges toward a vanishing point situated in the center of the painting, which thus deepens itself to infinity and leaves the visible, so to speak, draining itself into the white atom, from which the invisible literally swallows up the surrounding visible—and thus swallows up the gaze. Or as in his *Rubicon* (from 1969), where the surface spreads out red, splitting up according to two central vertical lines, the one announcing the other, characterized by obscurity, underlined by mauve strips, silently engulfed by an unspeakable but determined lack, the visible chromatic—pure depth from a black negativity. The invisible, in the end, can produce the visible in order to inscribe there paradoxically what the painting cannot give to be seen: movement. The techniques of *optical art* reach to the point where the gaze is in a panic that, being a centered and motionless aim [*visée*], it cannot envisage the entirety of the visible; this visible in fact destabilizes itself by the tricks of the invisible, which constructs it in voluntary contradiction with the psychological rules of perception, representation, and imagination, in such a way that the spectator must return there several times—for several looks—in order to see what nevertheless apparently gives itself as simply and purely visible, inert and flat. In fact, for example, in front of a canvas by Vasarely or one like *Physichromie* by Cruz-Diez (1981), the invisible destabilizes the visible in order to contradict the gaze—in order to put itself in movement, therefore, thanks to the immobility of the painting, that it might be seen. This ruse of the invisible testifies to the complete ideality of the visibly structured spectacle.

Nevertheless, the essential paradox of perspective, understood in the broad sense of the influence of the invisible on the visible, here still remains concealed. All that we have done to this point is transpose onto the painting the paradox that is already at work in natural vision: in both cases, the visible increases according to the measure of the invisible; space makes reality possible [*le vide rend possible le réel*]. However, in this second case, space [*le vide*] does not have the same status. In physical vision, I experience one perspective, in a space that allows me to see a distinguishable plurality of visible objects; thus, the perspective that is opened by the Triumphal Arch of the Carrousel welcomes into a fertile space the Concorde obelisk, then the Triumphal Arch of the Star; but this optical space corresponds to a real space: I can walk across the garden of Tuileries, go back up the Champs-Elysées, descend the avenue of the Great Army, to the point of the space formed by the Arche (square) of Defense—because here it is a matter of moving from the space of physical perspective to a space that is at the same time both phenomenological and real—an element of vision and a space inhabitable by a thing. Certainly the horizon (that is, the limit of perspective) continues to distance itself as I physically move myself toward it, by which it thoroughly escapes from the real; but this very escape does not forbid me, on the contrary, from actually moving—being a thing among things—in the space thus opened up. It is possible to walk in the perspective [of] Nievski, because it consists first of all in a thing, and second, only in a visible ideally submissive to the invisible. Conversely, the perspective that opens the painting will never be able to be physically traversed itself, because it remains first and uniquely ideal: the flatness of the painting physically allows for only length and breadth, not depth; with my finger (indeed on foot if it is a question of a monumental canvas), I am able to actually [*réellement*] run across the contours of the work, but I will never be able to initiate myself into the depths of the third dimension, which nevertheless, phenomenologically, I perceive first of all. So to the first paradox of perspective (the visible increases in direct proportion to the invisible), a second is added: the space that places the visible on stage or in view is not, in itself, real, in such a way that the real visible increases in direct proportion to a space of emptiness [*un vide de vide*].[13] In the painting, perspective does not open a single new dimension but *removes* a real dimension (the depth where I advance my steps) in order to—paradoxically!—reinforce by the same gesture both the closure of its surface and the indefinite staging of its levels. Sometimes the painting can open itself onto a physical perspective, as in *Clara-Clara*, in which Richard Serra arranged two arches of convergent circles at Tuileries, opening them onto the perspective of the triumphal arches; but precisely there the real perspective depended upon the irreal[14] perspective—and not the reverse: one entered into the physical perspective that much more when one first followed the irreal perspective. In a picture painted in accordance with the principles of perspective, the gaze has access to more of the visible than can be contained merely within the picture, if it appeared as only a pure object in space: the visible can accumulate itself and organize itself there without confusion only insofar as the invisible subjects it to ideality, and, first of all, subjects the painting to this same ideality. It is therefore necessary, in principle, that the invisible respect the ideality that it places in a work, thus that it produce space under the irreal and phenomenological mode of a space of emptiness [*un vide du vide*]—a space that is itself irreal. The point is not that, with perspective finally accomplished, we are dealing with an illusion, since in that respect, the painting welcomes more reality under the irreal mode (intentionally) than it could ever admit in terms of its physical flatness: perspective takes the gaze out of the picture, or more precisely, takes the picture out of its status of being a *tabula rasa*, closed in upon its flatness. The point is not a *trompe l'oeil*—a confusion between physical perspective and irreal perspective—since the eye sets itself straight [*se détrompe*] by refusing to give in to the appearance of the painting as a mere *tabula rasa*, a spatial object among others, in order to see, by an invisible transpiercing, nothing less than a world, a world within the world, a world sometimes more visible than the real world. It is a matter then—with the space of emptiness [*le vide du vide*], the power of the invisible on the visible that is at work in the placement in perspective—of opening up the flatness of the art-object onto and into a world: the invisible, in perspective, mundanizes [*mondanise*] a real visible by an infinite number of irreal visibles, and thereby renders the visible all the more apparent. "This is what must first be given to the painting, a harmonious warmth, an abyss into which the eye sinks, a voiceless germination" (Cézanne).[15]

III

Perspective manages to see to the traversal only so long as the painting is not able to see itself as such. Without the work of the invisible, what we perceive as visible actually would offer only a rhapsodic spectacle and confusion of colored spots. In fact "a painting—before being a battle horse, a nude woman or any particular thing—is essentially a flat surface covered with colors in a certain assembled order"; therefore to transform this flat surface covered with color, merely a physical object and effectively perceived given [*donnée effectivement perçue*], into a "horse battle" or what have you—that is to say, in order simply to see what is there to be seen—the visible must be constituted [*se former*], taking form thanks to the invisible. Every painting presents, in fact, an anamorphosis: the real given and actually perceived has no form so long as the gaze does not find the conditions and the point of view from which it takes shape for the first time. The anamorphosis—this complicated perspective, this simplified anamorphosis—attests to the fact that only the invisible makes possible the visible, by informing it: crossing over [*traverser*], the flatness of the real painting, though without ever exiting, in view of the spectacle aimed by the invisible gaze.

A similar distinction can be expressed in terms of Husserlian phenomenology. (a) The painting, as a real [*réel*] object and representation of itself, is proportionate to the experiences [*vécus*] of consciousness; since these define consciousness more than the eventual object of this consciousness, the visible of the painting gives nothing more to see than the flatness of the support, the arbitrariness of distorted forms, the rhapsody of colored spots; in short, and literally, the painting, like consciousness, resembles nothing. (b) Perspective, the product of a gaze that, by the space of emptiness [*le vide du vide*], deepens the given reality of the *tabula rasa* by the invisible impulse "into which the eye sinks," is equivalent to the aim of intentionality; in the end, the perspectival gaze is always a gaze of something other than what it actually experiences, in the same way that consciousness is always consciousness of something, thus of something other than itself. (c) The final spectacle—in the sense of the last visible to which the gaze leads in its placement in a finished form—that is to say, the completely deployed object (depth, levels, organization in space, etc.), indicates at the same time a definite irreality, equivalent to the intentional object but never perceived as such, for being completely irreal (intentional inexistence), it attains its form and visibility according to an aim that stretches or distends the experiences in view of some object and interprets them as this object; the intentional object results from a production of experience by intentionality, in the same way that the perspectival spectacle results from the production of the visible by the invisible.

In accordance with these phenomenological parallels, even the most realist of paintings must make visible what cannot be seen, and it can never—even if it wants to, it is not able to—make it simply visible. For in order to see a spectacle, it is necessary that the perceived visual given [*le donné visual perçu*] be subjected to a phenomenological (or perspectival) interpretation as an intentional object (or last spectacle). Contrary to what might be expected, nonrepresentational art is no exception to this interpretation in view of an intentional object; only in this case, the object aimed at appears neither in empirical nature nor in its elementary modulations, but in the field of the mind's imaginations of the possible: intentional objects still never aimed at, but nevertheless incontestable. The painting thus plays between the two extremes of intentionality: the lived experiences [*vécus*], perceptions, founded [*éprouvés*] and real, on the one hand, and the aimed-at intentional object seen invisibly and ideally on the other. The gaze, which exercises the phenomenological function of intentionality in order to see the ultimate object through these experiences, interprets the sensible visible as an irreal but accomplished object. Intentionality sees its object through the lived experiences [*les vécus*]—perspective crosses the visible to the invisible—in order to see all the more. The gaze, in both cases, sees in depth.

IV

Certain extreme (but nevertheless perhaps inevitable) gestures of painting can be deduced, or at least can be conceived, on the basis of this conceptual operation. The tension between the two axes of perspective, understood as the phenomenological distance between the experience of consciousness and the intentional (i.e., objective) object, offers the model of the tension between the two causes of perspective and thus of the painting it organizes. For the painting disappears according to perspective when one of the two factors in tension, lived experience [*vécu*] or the object, disappears.

On the one hand: a disappearance of the objective, when the experience itself becomes directly the end of the painting and the only visible. When Monet rendered the tower of the Parliament in London, though it did not disappear in the mist, it nevertheless was drowned by it; he made it sink into the painting itself, which closes itself to all invisible depth, to the exclusive profit of conscious facts, lived experiences and "impressions"; the tower sinks into no other fog than that fog of its own perception by the gaze; the tower itself withdraws in the face of the tower that is perceived; in place of the abolished tower, the gaze substitutes the experienced [*éprouvée*] tower; the aimed-at spectacle allows the depth of the painting to close itself in order to return to the *tabula rasa*, the clean slate, a flat deposit of the effectively lived experience. The gate of the Cathedral of Rouen does not appear to the different lights of even a solar day; on the contrary, even more so at the height of midday, it does not cease to disappear; and less by an experience of bedazzlement[16] than by a perfectly deposited trick [*trop*]; to speak of bedazzlement implies in effect that one always aims at an object and deplores, consequently, that the excess of light prevents a clear view. But here, the point is not to see, across this excess of light, the intentional object of a cathedral; it is a matter of receiving this light itself, as perceived, in the place and at the place of all illuminated objectivity. We will permit a painter to comment on the phenomenological situation of this painter, Monet:

In approaching Monet's *Cathédrale de Rouen*, they [*i.e.*, the spectators] also squint their eyes, wanting to find the contours of the cathedral, but the blurred spots did not express in any distinct way the forms of the cathedral. . . . One made the original suggestion to hang a photograph nearby, for the colors are given by the painter, but the photograph can provide the design, and the illusion will be complete. But the person was not seeing the painting itself, was not seeing the colored spots, did not see them grow in an infinite manner, and [did not see that] Monet, who painted this cathedral, strove to render the light and the shadow that were on the walls of the cathedral. It was not the light and the shadows that were his principal task, but the painting that was located in the shadow and in the light.[17]

We suspend, for a moment, the two final phrases, and hold onto what "is false" (for Malévitch the suprematist) but without doubt even less partially true for Monet. To render the light, render the shadow, thus make visible what, according to the simple gaze (and also perspective), remains a milieu of vision, not an objectivity; to establish the invisible in an objective visible—this paradoxical objectivity of impressionism demands in return that the generally visible objectivity disappear from the visible. And it cannot sink into the invisible, any more than this invisible itself that has become visible (as an intentional object) can become invisible again, because the invisible (the milieu, the immediately sensed experience [*le vécu immédiatement éprouvé*]) has deposed the visible. In this continual coming-and-going or appearing-withdrawal [*chassé-croisé*], the painting suspends what Husserl calls the principle of phenomenological correlation—namely, that each experience [*vécu*] of consciousness is intentionally related to an object that, thanks to this intentionality alone, concentrates itself in the visible, precisely because it puts into play the invisible authority. Monet did not understand this to be merely an originality of pictorial technique, an innovation in the psychology of perception or the opening up of a new visual field (although it does accomplish this as well); he understood it as one of the two principles for the destruction of phenomenological objectivity, carried out by granting exclusive privilege to one of its poles—the intentional experience [*le vécu intentionnel*].

Since the experience [*vécu*] of consciousness is invested exclusively in the totality of the visible (at least initially) and hence in every (intentional) distance between consciousness and something it intends as an object, some effects follow from this. The *Nympheas* inundates the eye, to the point of saturating every perception: the gaze does not cease to turn itself around in order to attempt, with minimal failure, to face up to the bluish assault of the perceivable; the gaze fights with itself while striving to perceive as much as it possibly can; the visible sets itself up in defiance of the gaze, which sees the excess of the perceptible only in repeated acts. Monet thus certainly anticipates the *tout autour* ("all over") canvas of Pollock: the painter floods colors and lines, in jumps, on an immense canvas, taken to be the ground; in fact it is no longer a matter of a canvas, since the painter walks over and traverses it, and then will carve it up afterward into various fragments, setting it up on a frame in order to create a canvas in the academic sense of the term. The painting thus takes place before the fabric loaded with pigments becomes the painting object, because the object of the painting not only does not anymore have anything to do with an intentional object, but therefore does not have any need of, nor right to, a painting objectifying the experience [*vécu*] as an intentional object. The painting is confined only to itself, that is, to the consciousness of the visible, a consciousness that feels [*éprouve*] and goes through the visible before all objectification (painting), because it is outside all objectivity (intentional object)—consciousness goes through and feels the visible in the very act of making visible the felt visible [*rendre visible le visible éprouvé*]; *action painting*[18] does not contradict this reduction of the painting to a collection of experiences of consciousness but rather completes it: the painting [*peignante*] consciousness requires not an object but simply the action of painting. Pollock, in walking on the canvas (which is not really one), accomplishes a trip not around his room but to the center of his consciousness. The painting consciousness becomes, to itself alone, without space or invisible, without intentionality or object, a world. And thus only that. The world of intentional objects dies in the action of painting, which already accomplishes a world in itself. Every form of "corporeal art" has recourse to this same privileging of the experience [*vécu*] of consciousness: the performance, a fortiori the nonrepeatable performance (self-mutilation, etc.), excludes not only the support of a painting (that is to say, the index of the perspectival operation) but above all the transcendence of an intentional object. In the body undertaking the action, the visible is reduced or minimized and is accomplished in the immediate experience of the visible by consciousness; or rather, on the contrary, it is a matter no longer of an experience [*vécu*] of the visible that is incorporated by consciousness but of seeing and making visible the experience of consciousness by the incorporation; in any case, the incorporating act identifies experience [*vécu*] and the visible, without intentionality, without support, without object.

V

On the other hand: although certainly in a way more difficult to conceive, the painting in accordance with perspective can disappear when it comes to lack not only an intentional object but the experience [*vécu*] as well. One sees this in one of the works that Hantaï rightly called *Tabula*, for example the one from 1974 found at the Museum of Modern Art in Paris. The serial regularity of 496 blue squares all almost identical, positioned in a rectangle that traverses, in order to separate them, 17 and 32 white columns and rows, setting up a mechanical production: folding the canvas according to the columns, which are coated with blue, then unfolding it, allowing the final operation to appear. The mechanistic element, moreover, does not decide anything: every painting implies a mechanics. What then must be read here? The mechanical production would, in every case, have been able to make another canvas larger than the present one (which is already 300 cm x 574 cm); should Hantaï's extension be interpreted in the sense of the efforts of Monet and Pollock? It would seem that precisely the opposite is being attempted: here, the canvas does not open itself as a world of consciousness, as a deposit of the overflow of the mundanized [*mondanisante*] consciousness, because the understanding remains purely repetitive, in the close contingency of the stripes of an accidental white on specifically identical squares; the enlargement of the *tabula* would neither apprehend nor show anything—so it remains, by definition, a *tabula rasa.*[19] The visible frees itself for itself, as contrary to the consciousness that perceives it, since in fact the gaze understands very quickly, in front of the canvas, "that there is nothing there to see"; or more precisely (for this formula would be better suited to the inverse orientation, where it is the intentional object that is lacking), the gaze understands that the visible has need only of a consciousness to experience it in order for it to be seen; the eye has nothing, or almost nothing, to experience [*éprouver*], to construct or put in perspective, since every visible, from itself and by its very poverty, has already accomplished its own placement in the scene: the minimum invisible already governs the visible, since it is a matter of a minimum visible; the white rows accentuate the blue squares automatically, without my gaze intervening, except to note its delayed vision. The reservation and insignificance of the visible guarantees that it has an autonomy with respect to every experience of consciousness, a consciousness reduced to observing what it no longer constitutes. The slogan of minimalist art indicates nicely the condition of a similar autonomy: the visible itself accomplishes the invisible *mise en scène* of every painting; the departure from perspectival consciousness demands that the retained intentional object mobilizes only the minimum of the invisible *mise en scène*: minimum, because beyond the visible it would no longer suffice to produce the invisible correspondent; minimum, because such a poverty confuses and distresses consciousness, to the point that it is rendered incapable of exercising the invisible. The autonomy of the intentional object with respect to the experiences [*les vécus*] (even intentional experiences) of consciousness makes possible the squares of Hantaï, but above all revives, through the "intermediary," let us say, of Josef Albers and his *Homage to the Square*, to the original *White Square on Black Base* of Malévitch. The doctrine is here explicitly made a part of the pictorial reasoning (if, at least, one can still speak of "painting" when it comes to suprematism): the square, first black on a white base (1915), then blue, finally white on a white base (1918), does not offer the visibility of any preexisting, worldly object, not even the analytic deconstruction that cubism effected (cubism remaining realism, indeed the most authentic of hyperrealisms); no interstice opens itself where the invisible can effect the slightest perspective, or the least constructivism (which marks the limits of any rapprochement between Malévitch and Léger). In this sense, the appearance of an object disappears, and it inevitably becomes necessary to speak of a painting without an object: "The picture is itself [*se fait*], but the object is not given. . . . The objects disappeared like smoke for a new artistic culture."[20] Is it necessary, furthermore, to fold back suprematism onto impressionism, and move the center of gravity of the intentional object of vision toward the experiences [*vécus*] of consciousness? Exactly the opposite would be correct, for the object stigmatized by nonobjectivity does not exactly correspond with the intentional object, which is unaware of its constitution, and thus of the autonomy that runs counter to consciousness, an autonomy that works against the intentionality that completely determines it in both cases. The autonomy of objective intentionality determines, on the contrary, in phenomenological language, that which constitutes the suprematist painting: the pure thing, issued from nothing other than its own invisibility, literally issued from nothing,[21] in complete independence of states of consciousness, whether that of the spectator or that of the painter: "It is necessary to construct in time and space a system that does not depend on any beauty, any emotion, any aesthetic state and that would be the philosophical system of color, where the new progresses of our representations, as a knowledge [*connaissance*], find themselves realized."[22] The square reproduces nothing, does not satisfy any aesthetic need, nor is it the deposit of the experiences of consciousness: "The square is a royal child full of life."[23] Such a "nonobjective phenomenon" carries out a "new realism of things"[24] by liberating the thing from every subjective edifice, to its full ownership of the invisible where its visibility resides, without alienating it as an act of the gaze. The white square on a white base has no need for any gaze, for any perspectival perspicacity in order to appear according to its intrinsic invisibility. The visible is liberated from vision at the moment when it seizes its own invisibility. The invisible, from that point on, plays no longer *between* the aim of the gaze and the visible but rather, contrary to the gazing aim, *in* the visible itself—and is merged with it, inasmuch as the white square is merged with its white base. Inasmuch: that is to say, not completely. Would this be the reason why we have spoken about it—even if spontaneously—since the first criticism of the first square (Alexandre Benois, scandalized besides), as an icon?

VI

Surpassing objectivity also requires undoing perspective, since both organize the gaze of the visible ordered according to the depth of the invisible. Their general disqualification thus implies the possibility of a new relation [*jeu*] between the visible and the invisible, where no longer is one or the other placed on stage, but both are placed there permanently. Or, we suggest, the invisible *in* the visible. It remains, that is, only if an insertion is effected similar to the suprematist and exemplary square, or if the painting has, already more or less, practiced elsewhere the insertion of the invisible in the visible. At this juncture, obviously, one thinks of the icon, which is exemplary in at least three traits.

First, the icon offers itself to be seen by the gaze without the mobilization of perspective. Certainly it does not in principle exclude a backdrop, sometimes precise and complex, or the organization of several outlines. And yet the economy of the icon does not depend upon the investment of space by the invisible; the invisible here plays a role more fundamental than the simple organization of space, a simple choreographing of the visible. The invisible is at play elsewhere and otherwise. Here we find the second decisive characteristic of the icon: it always shows a gaze belonging to a human face. This gaze, although painted as an invisible object, is its own [*a en propre de regarder*]; it sees more than is seen, not only because it is found painted most of the time in a central and facing position, but above all because, painted at the center of the icon, and ascribed to a saint, the Virgin, or Christ, this gaze looks at, outside of the icon and in front of it, the believer who is taken through the icon to the saint, the Virgin, or Christ. The gaze looks at the one who, in prayer [*orant*],[25] raises his gaze toward the icon: the painted gaze invisibly responds to the invisible gaze of the one in prayer, and transfigures its own visibility by including it in the commerce of two invisible gazes—the one from a praying man, taken through the painted icon, to look upon an invisible saint, the other the gaze of the invisible saint covered with benevolence, visible through the painted icon, looking upon the one in prayer. The invisible moves across the visible, in such a way that the painted icon supports the pigments less by the wood of its plank than by the liturgical and oratory exchange of gazes that meet one another there. The visible, what the painter himself by prayer deposits on wood, deploys itself saturated with the invisible of the exchanged gazes. The invisible is neither devoted to itself nor devoted to the service of the visible, as in perspective. On the contrary, it is the visible that serves the invisible, from which the real play, outside of every painting, in the end is freely exercised: the exchange of crossed [*croisé*] gazes of the one in prayer and Christ (or of his lieutenant) crossing through the visible—according to the holy economy of Creation and the Incarnation—but not itself contained there. Not "there" because, on a corporeal register, the gaze of our eyes always remains invisible: I can see a body, in all its nudity, and a face as objects placed in evidence and in a spectacle; I can never see the eyes of another human; or rather, even if I see his iris and so on, I cannot see his gaze, since it comes out of his pupils, which are empty spaces; the gaze alone is not real [*réel*]: it is born from a black hole, which, in the dialogue I look for or flee from, I want to capture or avoid, precisely because its irreal space fascinates me, as the source of the invisible, at the center of the visible. The icon pictorially depends upon the inclusion, in the human gaze, of the invisible within the visible, in order thus to establish subsequently, in a work, the spiritual exchange of the man praying to a benevolent God. The exchange of gazes (the one aiming in the way of the prayer, the other aiming in the way of benediction), in effect by crossing the visible, opens up to an extremely erotic face-to-face relation: two invisible gazes crossing themselves through the visible witness of their bodies.[26]

The icon—its third trait—effects the insertion of the invisible in the visible more radically than the suprematist *Square*. For the "nonobjective phenomenon," even if it goes straight to the invisible as the basis of the visible, still gives itself again to be seen and really inhabits the visible plane: we must learn to see the canvas as the presence of a nonobject, which nevertheless shares the complete visibility of objects; no phenomenological grounds can support us in the correct apprehension of the *Square* as invisible. On the contrary, the icon offers a phenomenological basis for its subversion of the visible by the invisible: the play of gazes, which crosses the painted visible in accordance with the economy of prayer and love, and which provokes the irreality that originates from them. The icon definitively withdraws itself from the objectivity of a spectacle dependent upon consciousness by overturning the relation between the spectator and the spectacle: the spectator discovers himself invisibly seen by the painted gaze of the icon, which, from that time on, appears as the treasure chest [*l'écrin*] of a central authority, never (by definition) painted and invisible—the gaze of the saint, the Virgin, or

Christ. In this situation, we have not exited from perspective because we still have not entered there: the invisible has better things to do, in painting, than to put the visible in place, indeed to denounce this placement in an objective scene (Malévitch). This, because the visible has, in painting as in reality, better things to do than be constituted in a spectacle, even in a spectacle governed by the invisible. The opening of a world should not be confused with the production of spectacles, even if it makes them possible. The trading [*commerce*] of the visible with the invisible does not exhaust itself in perspective, which merely constitutes, on the contrary, a particular case, and, despite its overabundant richness, has become otherwise exhausted. It may be that the trading of the visible with the invisible has been understood as symbolic of another exchange—and not necessarily the one that Kant privileged.

Let us leave undecided what, in any case, we could not even approach here. What is required is to openly oppose the two games where visible and invisible can cross themselves. Or better, the invisible emerges between the gaze and the visible, from which it [the invisible] places the visible on stage in order to serve it: it [the invisible] results in perspective, a classical phenomenological situation of objective intentionality, and two contrary directions to contest it. Or better, the invisible is exerted as the gaze itself, which invisibly gazes upon another invisible gaze through the intermediary of a painted visible, which enshrines these invisibles as the iris surrounds the pupil; the invisible then freely plays and liberates the visible from the status of spectacle; the result is a phenomenological situation that is less classical, where intentionality is no longer fulfilled by an objectivity, indeed is fulfilled owing to its own status as an *I.* This dilemma can be put to the test in the face of each painting: it is only a matter of finding it or the gazes, and to question itself on only one point: Do these gazes offer themselves to be seen as objects (in that case, they would be taken in a perspective, as is every other object), or better, do they offer themselves as aims addressed to the spectator (in that case, they would transgress all placement in scene [*mise en scène*], perspectival or not)? In the majority of paintings, the decision does not offer any difficulty. There is, however, a type that is trickier: portraits. Certainly, most treat the gaze of the model as a visible object, above all when magnificence and dignity demand a complex *mise en scène,* thus a perspective.

There remains a privileged subset, where the undecidability perhaps encounters itself: self-portraits. In this case, we know that the painter has painted the invisible from one gaze at least—his own—and that this gaze looked at it and looked at looking at it [*il l'a regardé et regardé le regardant*]; that the crossing of the invisible (gazes) has therefore indeed taken place; and that the visible, here, at least on this occasion, was not the goal; moreover, most often, that the perspective disappears. Do we nevertheless always have an icon? Certainly not with the rare self-portraits of Picasso (such as the one from Bremen, dated 1965), who recalls, "Really I didn't frequent my face very much";[27] so also in the *Portrait of Cézanne* at the Louvre we find Cézanne himself treated like his other subjects following the example of a landscape, from which the depth sculptures itself by the calibration of tones, and where the gaze itself dissolves in the eyes, homogenous to the other dark flat surfaces. There is a gaze that actually regards itself, on the contrary, in the prodigious self-portrait by Dürer (1500, Ancient Gallery, Munich): facing the spectator, face-to-face with the painter of the painting himself, in majesty, in the position of Christ. Does this nevertheless act as an icon? Probably not, and not only because of the blasphemy, quiet, unconscious maybe, but more obviously, for investing the christic site and for claiming to become oneself the center of an icon; for, more essentially, the icon exchanges two invisible gazes, that of the one in prayer [*orant*] and that of the benevolent one; here, a single gaze attempts to play both roles; the gaze of the painter does not exchange itself with any other invisible but deposits itself in visibility to become its own spectacle. For this gaze, captured in the visible face, no invisible breaks in to the ideal authority of the act of painting, that of an object in perspective, either to us or to Dürer, who does not see himself; instead he finds that he has merely inverted his own face, symmetrically, as the mirror demands it. The invisible that invests the visible according to an icon remains itself forever and at first sight other than the invisible of my own gaze. In painting, as elsewhere, the invisible is received but not produced.

2

What Gives

I

In order to see, we have no need for painters, at least in order to see what already gives itself to be seen—available, affected, fitted to its seizure by a gaze. Either because the thing naturally belongs to the visible wealth that the world incessantly gives to us, or because our gaze, confident in its own powers or at least aided by mechanical devices, manages the stores of the visible—in either case, we still have no need of painters. One then casts glances [*regards*] around oneself as though one were the owner of a tower, with the stupid serenity of calm possession, which suspects neither the catastrophic nor the perduring deception of things. The spectacle of the visible already given in the scattered labyrinth of everyday sight can only evade the barely vigilant guard mounted in front of it by my wearied and satisfied eye. One knows what one sees and what one must see; one assures oneself that only what one sees coincides with what one must see, in a calm possession, without search, without surprise.

If therefore we have recourse, at least sometimes, to the indirect, deceptive, and optional spectacle of a painting, if we entrust our eye to the eye of a painter, as though one were following in the footsteps of a guide, this would thus only be in order to see something other than what is visible to us. We look at what is offered by the painter only in order to see a visible that remains inaccessible to our vision. For if he paints what he sees—himself—he nevertheless does not paint what, as a rule, *we* see at first sight (our own). The painter sees and so gives to be seen what without him would remain forever banished from the visible. The painting does not manage the organization of the visible by otherwise combining what is already seen: it adds to the mass of already-seen or possibly anticipated phenomena an absolutely new phenomenon, still not seen. It is said that a painting, before offering to the gaze—as an intentional object—a woman, a tree, or a fruit, actually and first of all must produce a surface for the support and accumulation of paste. But that is an understatement. The painting—at least one that is authentic—imposes in front of every gaze an absolutely new phenomenon, increasing by force the quantity of the visible. The painting—the authentic one—exposes an absolutely original phenomenon, newly discovered, without precondition or genealogy, suddenly appearing with such a violence that it explodes the limits of the visible identified to that point. The painter, with each painting, adds yet another phenomenon to the indefinite flow of the visible. He completes the world, precisely because he does not imitate nature. He deepens a seam or fault line, in the night of the inapparent, in order to extract, lovingly or more often by force, with strokes and patches of color, blocks of the visible.

II

With the painting, the painter, like an alchemist, makes visible what without him would have remained definitively invisible. We shall call this the *unseen* [*l'invu*]. The unseen is not seen, just as the unheard-of [*l'inouï*] is not heard, the unknown [*l'insu*] is not known, indeed just as the disgusting is not appreciated [or the disgusting cannot be stomached]. The unseen admittedly falls under the jurisdiction of the invisible, but it should not be confused with it, since it is able to transgress it precisely by becoming visible; while the invisible remains forever as such—recalcitrantly irreducible to the *mise en scène*, to the apparition, to the entrée into the visible—the unseen, only provisionally invisible, always exerts its demand for visibility in order to be made to irrupt, sometimes by force, onto the scene. The unseen has only been prevented from suddenly appearing in the visible. It holds there all of its desire, as though tortured by the excess of what it knows it is able to offer to the glory of the gaze. By waiting and by desiring to appear, the unseen remains, as such, unseen—at least as long as each *mise en forme* is not put on display [*aussi longtemps du moins qu'aucune mise en forme ne le met en scène*]. Aristotle spoke of the desire of ὕλη [matter] for form, and compared this to the example of the female desire for the male; except that the female imposes on the male by the prestige of her form and rays of visible splendor, so that the unseen suffers precisely from its continued nonappearance in any form and desires only access to a mode of appearance. And at the same time, the ὕλη [matter] itself remains unknown as such, according to Aristotle, owing to a lack of proper visibility; it comes out only by analogy with the form that it is not and without which its obscurity remains irremediable. The unseen, shapeless [*informe*] material and yet to be seen, from which springs all visibility, desires its placement in form [*mise en forme*].

The porter who filters the unseen's access to the visible, the master of every entrée onto the scene, the guardian of the limits of appearance is called the painter. Plato was not mistaken to denounce the painter as being at the same time earthly [*tellurique*] and Apollonian, a figure who delights in advancing to the higher office of philosophy—that of determining presence. Only the painter grants the *venia apparendi*, the license to appear, the right to presence. The painter grants visibility to the unseen, delivering the unseen from its anterior invisibility, its shapelessness [*l'informe*]. But why is it the painter who manages to do this—he and he alone? How does he seize the power to make the unseen appear? By what gift [*grâce*] does one become a painter? Certainly it is not enough to be able to see, to be on duty with a gaze, so to speak, to have an eye (*inteuri, in-tueri, re-garder*) for the visible already available and on display every day, since in that case every nonblind person would know how to paint. If the painter rules over the access of the unseen to the visible, his gift thus has nothing to do with his vision of the visible but with his divination of the unseen [*l'invu*]. The painter, like the blind man, sees more than the visible, painting and seeing par excellence. The painter allows his gaze to wander in obscurity on this side of the visible, slipping under the line of visibility, positioned just under the watermark of the visible—as in subwork [*sous-oeuvre*], in the darkened hold of the visible that still saturates the unseen. Thus, in vessels of old, the deepest hold, far beneath the watermark line, always remained filled with sea water. It is even to that point that the blind gaze of the painter descends: he is lost in the unseen, in order to locate there what waits only for him to bring it up to the full sun of visibility. The painter works in the obscure chaos [Genesis 1:2] that precedes the separation of the waters below and the waters above [Genesis 1:7], the distinction between the unseen [*l'invu*] and the visible. He works before the creation of the first light [Genesis 1:3]. He goes back to the creation of the world, half witness, half archangel-laborer. There is also the risk that in finishing the work he will lose himself, as if, by going back before the separation of the waters, before the separation of light from darkness, he has also gone back before the distinction between good and evil. For, certainly more than any of the other arts, painting directly and essentially involves a matter of moral choice.

The painter descends to the undecidable frontier of the visible and the unseen only in order to cross it himself. Feeling his way, one by one, he leads the unseens [*les invus*] from archaic obscurity to the light of visibility. Within the setting of a frame, he brings up such an unseen to the light of day. He must consider the frame where the painting rests to be the gate of the Underworld—the one from which arises, still blind, but miraculously snatched from the reign of darkness, a new visible, which up to that point has remained unseen. Each painting gives us a Eurydice, saved (and not lost) because she was seen, even though she remained unseen to everyone other than the nightly diurnal eye of painter. Orpheus did not sing; he painted. Or better, he saw in the unseen what the shroud of darkness could not hide, with its mute and powerless requirement to appear. He understood, from the vigilance of his benevolent gaze, the anxious desire to appear. The eye loves nothing more than the ear: for it grants to the unseen its salvation, under the protection of a gaze that still sees nothing. So it was not for nothing that the early Christians claimed the title of Orpheus for Christ, who led the captives out of Hades [Ephesians 4:8]. Every painting participates in a resurrection, every painting imitates Christ, by bringing the unseen to light. And if the painter sinks so far below the line of visibility as to find there an absolutely new visible—without exemplar, model, or precedent—none of our calmly assured spectacles of their reposed visibility would be able to guide it, nor determine what is finally going to appear—perhaps because no one is able to *see* ahead [pré *voir*]. The painter must lose himself in order to be saved (and to escape). Like Christ, he is neither welcomed nor saved, because he first gives himself, without ever knowing in advance if he will lose himself or be saved. The painter is not necessarily damned, but he is always ordained [*consacré*].

The unseen that the painter will look for thus remains, up to the point of its final appearance, unforeseen [*imprévu*]—unseen, thus unforeseen. The unseen, or the unforeseen par excellence. Like death, which (in principle) is not here so long as I am here, the unseen remains *inapparent* as long as it is, and disappears the moment that it appears as visible. The unseen appears only in order to disappear as such. Further, one is not able in any way to foresee the new visible in terms of its unseen, which is by definition invisible. Only the painter can sense this transition, more than he can see it, and he can say nothing, since to show it would be to mask it. Producing a painting is thus never the equivalent of rendering real a "preseen" [or previously seen] visibility, preconceived and already seen before suddenly appearing in the light to be perceived. In that sense, every production would be reduced to a mere *re*production, or the really [*effectivement*] visible would be limited to the power of the visible. Academicism [in art] consists only in this: claiming to foresee a painting, the painter prohibits the sudden appearing of the unseen and instead fixes its shape at first sight. In this respect, academicism is encountered in many different painters and in every period, no less our own than past epochs. It could even be said that conceptual art offers the exemplary and definitive model of academicism, not only because the visible itself is defined by the concept—by some exterior understanding in advance—but above all because the work itself cannot and must not appear as such.[1] *Ready-made* art, on the contrary, does complete justice to the unforeseen [*imprévu*] appearance of the work, since it takes up the object that was seen before as being completely defined by its banal usage and mass production and resituates it, so to speak, in the unexpected [*l'imprévisible*], or better, in the unseen [*l'invu*]. Between the store and the museum, the bottle holder has taken a bath in the unseen, and its absolutely new visibility has no other legitimacy than the fact that it has just made it through. The *ready-made* makes an impression not so much because it is blatantly banal as because it has been immunized from such banality by being bathed in the unseen, and then, indeed especially, because it reemerges, visible among the visibles. Baptized by the unseen, but also saved from the waters of the unseen, the visible painting lives on a resuscitated life—new, pardoned [*grâciée*], imprescriptible. Thus the visible imitates nothing other than itself. The painting lives as human beings do: singularly, for itself, unique and irreplaceable [*insubstitutablement*]. The true painter shares the simple mystery of the one Creation, in that he reproduces nothing, but *pro*duces. Or rather ushers something from the unseen into the visible in order thus to inseminate—sometimes by a violation[2]—the sterile reproduction of the visible by itself, which one commonly calls "creation." Especially and above all in more classical painters, a violence seizes the debased visible exhausted by reproduction, in order to accentuate it under the guidance of radically unseen lines and saturate it with a novelty ushered in from the unseen, as in the work of Caravaggio, Vouet, and El Greco. The true painting does not rise[3] from one visible to another but implores the visible already seen to allow itself to be increased and opened by a new glory. The unseen takes up the visible [*l'invu remonte au visible*]: it climbs toward the visible. But above all, the unseen teaches the visible a thing or two [*l'invu en remontre au visible*]: it reveals [*montre*] the visible and imposes upon it that of which the visible remained still unaware, protesting the moribund equilibrium by the immigration of a barbaric force. The gates of Hell fly open without ceasing, from which the painter returns to the light of day as a new master of the visible, who climbs back up only to teach us a thing or two and, in fact, show us a monster [*nous montrer un monstre*]. *Monstrum,* the presentable [*le montrable*] par excellence, the brute unseen, the miracle. *Miraculum,* the admirable par excellence. The painter of miracles is made to blink when encountering the visible too much foreseen.

III

When the unseen is uncovered, as an absolutely new appearance [*venu*] in the visible, this implies that it imposes itself there in perfect independence. The painting, if it is authentic, visibly imposes itself. Visibly: it must impose itself without discussion and by force, but with the sole authority of the evidence of the visible, or rather of the unseen that has become visible. And moreover, it is with an obvious complacent readiness to oblige that it places itself on the stage of visibility; it aspires to be there and consents to be there with a visible pleasure. This gift for making itself seen does not result from the propensity of visitors to come to see it; the painting does not become visible because we go to visit it, called in groups, attentive or distracted. We visit it, on the contrary, because its intrinsic visibility imperatively calls [*convoque*] us—just as it is necessary to visit prisoners and the sick, who retain a right to company despite their fate; and just as it is necessary and inevitable to end up yielding to the desire of seeing again and receiving back the one whom one loves, simply because he remains there, waiting for an homage that is owed him, although distance and customs may oppose it. By filing past the painting, we do not consume it as prey for the eyes, since, willingly or unwillingly, knowing it or not, we do not grant it the magisterial homage that it rightfully deserves—even commands. Moreover, when the real visibility [*la visibilité effective*] finds itself arbitrarily compromised by loss, flight, alteration, or simply being locked up in the cellar (what happens, fundamentally, when a painting finds itself put in reserve, such an unintelligible attack upon its inalienable right to be seen, as a survivor from the unseen?), our gaze still strains toward it because, in itself and by right, its fate intrinsically consists in being seen—*videndum*, coming to be seen. The authentic [*véritable*] painting inspires the look of its visitors, [but] not because it inhales it from the depths of the unseen from which it arises continually; it does not inhale [*aspire*] it, because it exudes [*respire*] visibility from top to bottom. The unseen, in the painting, exudes visibility, just as one is a "picture of health" [*on respire la santé*], but also as a captive liberated by a miracle exudes liberty. Having escaped from the unseen, the painting breathes in the air of the light of day, the liberty of appearance. The unseen breathes in [*respire*]—more than every other spectacle born in a visibility so common that it no longer even recognizes it—the air and space of liberated visibility, because it attains such only with difficulty and for an instant. The painting still enjoys a mere resident's permit in the light of day, as an aesthetic refugee. Still dripping with the formless and colorless obscurity of the ὕλη [matter] from which it was born with difficulty, as though covered in amniotic fluid, the unseen enters through the space of the frame into the royal court of visibility, ascending to the throne of an unhoped-for evidence—radiating. By forced entry, it bursts into the field henceforth definitively opened up to the visible, where, by contrast, it shines with the dazzling, irrepressible brilliance of those who have been miraculously saved [*des miraculés*],[4] *miraculum* itself, phenomenon par excellence. The last unseen, henceforth transformed into and by visibility, raises it to a degree of intensity hitherto unknown—or more precisely, unseen.

This is why, according to sound logic, each painting must effect two contradictory attractions upon its spectators. First, of course, the fascination of the gaze by the irresistible attraction of its weight of glory. But also terror in the face of the power that it exerts in the name of the darkness from which it arises. The picture has transgressed the most forbidden border: it comes to us from the unseen, by forced entry, illegally, heroic and threatening; it has seen what cannot be seen—namely, the unseen; it still bears the marks of the forbidden, despite having renounced it. The authentic painting defies us, provokes us, sometimes with the mischievous arrogance of some upstart who has reached visibility, more rarely with the royal and sacerdotal holiness of a master of appearance. To think about it properly, it would be necessary to be purified before entering into its presence. For glory threatens, even when it saves.

IV

It follows that the authentic painting registers itself in the visible only by being ordered to be there, as though by a commander. For, more than any other visible, the one miraculously saved from the unseen knows the difference between invisibility and visibility. It has paid the price for such knowledge. Consequently, no painter worthy of the title would attempt to control the painting as a—or his—object. To bring his work to life only in order to make it his slave or mistress: this would be enough to disqualify a painter as such. The true painter does not know what he painted, and devoted his knowledge only to begging for the surprise of discovering what he had not dared to foresee. The whole mastery consists, precisely, in ultimately letting the unseen burst into the visible by surprise, unpredictably. The instant when the unseen appears—piercing the surface of visibility from the obscure abyss—coincides precisely with its complete emancipation from its guardian, its coach, its smuggler—the painter. If the painting were to remain obedient to its painter—useless servant, vanquished master—after its publication, it would immediately lose its glory as the one miraculously saved from the unseen. It would recede to the rank of a simple object, ordered to the agreeable and convenient vision for consumption. Here we mean to include the painters of "series," "periods," or "manners," masters (small or big, it matters little, for if they only master, they lose everything), the quaint artists of the pleasant [*les artistes d'agrément*], of function and of design (selling, sold): in every case, their gazes dominate the visible; consequently they produce and reproduce (themselves); but by dominating the visible, they appropriate it, thus reducing it to their measure, and so destroy it. One wishes to see the painting, but one sees only a man, him or myself. Conversely, the [authentic] painter refrains from seeing what he wants in order to let what he does not want be seen, since he is no longer attempting (nor tempted) to be able to make (or to see) that which he is still able to desire or master. He is trying to let burst onto the scene much more than what is predelineated [*prévu*], more than what is seen, more than what he desires or wills. Or rather, he does what he wants—lets an unseen appear (thus immediately disappear as such) in the realm of visibles—only by abandoning the production of what he could nevertheless perfectly effectuate: a predelineated object. Only thus does he allow something that resembles nothing else suddenly to appear, [something] that has neither meaning [*sens*] nor the slightest utility, in short a new view [*vu*], a new coming [*venu*] in the visible, recovered from the unseen and in terms of its lost origin. The authentic painting fulfills the expectation of the painter and the visitor, strictly speaking, by surprising it, disorienting it, and flooding it. It fills not the expected expectation but rather another expectation—the unexpected. Its reality [*effectivité*] does not accomplish an already-defined possibility; it opens up a possibility to that point not anticipated, unthinkable, impossible. Not that such a picture robs itself of our desire to see: it robs us of our very meager desire—prudent and restricted—to see only what we had foreseen in all its quotiddity, in order to open us up to a pure desire to see otherwise [*autrement*] and something other than what we expected but would never be able to see and await.

The authentic painting annuls our desire in order to give rise to a new one, according to the measure of what thus becomes aimed-at [*visable*].[5] For the visible, largely unanticipated, must itself provoke the aim [intention] that renders it accessible and bearable for eyes previously half-closed. The visible precedes the aim: this is what must be rendered *visable* by us, since we did not expect it. Coming among its own, it had to note that its own did not foresee it and therefore rendered itself [or surrendered itself to being] *visable* by them.[6] The painting must train us to see it. The distance between the idol and the icon is defined here. The idol still remains, in one way or another, proportionate to the expectation of the desire; thus it fulfills (sometimes to a degree more than expected) the anticipation. The icon definitively exceeds the scope of expectation, terrifying the desire, annulling the anticipation: it is neither willing nor able to undertake to correct this gap; the icon inverts it while substituting its own aim—its aim toward us—in place of ours toward it. But one should not be deceived: for the painting to reach the rank of an idol is already a remarkable achievement. For the idol, a first visible not overtaken by a gaze, arrests and fills the gaze. It freezes in an invisible mirror: the gaze is proportioned to the idol, from which it learns—in the same way that an echo that is sent back to a radar works to situate one in space—to the extent that it is allowed to fill it. The authentic painting would not give itself to be seen in such glory if it had not taken and surprised our scope of expectation. We depend more upon it, in gazing upon it, than it does upon us.

V

What painting remains, in this sense, possible today? If out of this discussion comes a single clear lesson about the evolution of contemporary painting, perhaps it is this: the autonomous glory of the painting has disappeared.

Certainly the luxuriance of visible spectacles has not disappeared—quite the contrary. But what has disappeared is the authority of the work that suddenly appears and bursts forth from the unseen into the visible. And in at least two ways. On the one hand, the painting limits itself to being a mere recording, simply recording the most fitting private impressions or spectacles for the desiring gaze, like so many experiences of consciousness being set forth in order to be read, indeed, on the support and the surface, but, by right, completely enslaved to the consciousness that consigns them there. This line of development is seen from Monet to Pollock through Matisse and Masson, and it is precisely this path that leads the way into the impasse of *action painting*[7] and performance art. Here, no unseen origin, no genesis toward the visible, no transformation can assure the painting of an autarchic authority derived from its own glory. It does not intrude upon sight, since it is the gaze that forces itself to appear as it appears, merely representing the desire to be seen or to make itself seen; it no longer concentrates the piety of the gaze, neither itself nor the created one, since it merely records—with the scrupulous modesty of a security clerk—the depths of a desire for the spectacle that no longer promises any pleasure—indeed disgusts it.[8] On the other hand, conversely, the painting effectively disappears even though it still exists after having been stripped of all visible glory. Like the *tabula rasa*, like the monochrome squares, like the black diagonal lines on a surface, like all of the installations of conceptual art, the painting gives to be seen what, in the visible—an intentional object stripped of every experience of consciousness—presents itself is not merely as "not visible": thanks to the painting, the experience [*preuve*] is created in which there is no longer anything to see. It is necessary to circulate; the gaze circulates thus, abandoning the depleted thing, put in its place by so many other concepts of the object, like all the other depleted "visibles." The visible thus sinks in the conception.[9]

It could be that the current crisis of painting demonstrates a crisis of the visible itself. This crisis of the visible would result from the pressure exerted upon the unforeseen appearance of the unseen in the visible by the strictly technical model of production of the visible according to the logic of anticipation [*prévu*]. The technical project manages the forms according to the multiform expectation [*prévision*] of desire—responding to long-term anticipated analyzed needs, the projected result of free markets or profits, investments made in anticipation of the developments of the market, advancement in research, and so on. In this context, how can the unanticipated, the seal of the conversion from the unseen to the visible, retain its possibility?

Even the master painter betrays, to a certain degree by the refusal of asceticism, the impasse or aporia of painting itself. Here also—here above all—the principle that "all that can be made must be made" leads to death by an entropy of insignificance. By yielding to this principle shamelessly and without reservation, painting today, as previously with other principles (the principle of sufficient reason, or of subjectivity, among others), has anticipated the exact sciences. But for this pertinence it has paid an exorbitant price: the loss of nonmastery, or better, the inversion of mastery, shifting from the unseen [*l'invu*] to the anticipated [*prévu*]. From this we can consider the symbolic influence upon this [past] century of painting exercised by Picasso, the most extraordinary creator of the foreseen [*prévu*], the one most deadly for the unforeseen [*l'imprévu*], therefore of the miracle. How to return and recognize, henceforth, a radical origin of the painting—granting to it again the radically original dignity of the visible? How to return to its edges, to wait for it, in the patience of the work that suddenly appears, streaming again from the unseen, the visible in glory?

VI

That the painting should appear from itself—here is the absurdity par excellence. The painting, like every work (of art or not), is born from work, from a worker, from the travail of an other. The painting belongs to its author, whom it reflects.

This obvious fact, however, does not hold. The authentic painting—and this is the unique motif of the fascination that it exerts upon its spectator—escapes as much the one who signs it as the one who looks at it. Moreover, many among them do not carry any signature; just as many have crossed centuries without any gaze that could render to them either justice or respect. Authentic paintings suddenly appear to cross the eyes of painters and spectators, but by preceding and determining, far from submitting themselves to them. Why? Because the painting offers the frame that is the site of the sudden appearance of lines, shapes, and colors—none of which were predestined to appear as they do. On their surface absolutely unforeseen lines etch themselves, imposing themselves from their necessity. The truly creative painter, then, is characterized not by a plastic inventiveness imposing his will but rather by a passive receptivity, which, from among a million equally possible lines, knows to choose this one that imposes itself from its own necessity. An old adage claims that the sculptor contents himself with merely eliminating, from the block of stone, the superfluous masses that prevent its form from appearing in its proper splendor. In the same way, certainly, the painter contents himself with merely eliminating the lines and colors that, by their arbitrariness, conceal or distort the sudden autonomous appearance of the unseen, such that it demands, from itself alone [*à partir de lui seul*], to attain to appearance. As a blind man feels the contours of the ground with his cane, the painter feels the not yet visible with his brush, in order to pinpoint there, among all of the geometrically possible lines (for all of them are by right, all can have an equation, equally rational, therefore equally traceable), the one that obeys an indisputable aesthetic necessity. The painter traces nothing. He only pinpoints, like one divining water, what can (and therefore must) well up from below. He guesses [*devine*], better than the blind daily march of observers [*les aveugles quotidiennement voyants*], what claims to reach the visible by virtue of the pressure of the unseen. The painter does not trace any lines, nor does he define any form. He allows the forms and features to impose themselves upon the surface in the frame—first preserved outside the visible that is already assigned to other possessors—in the neutral *templum* of the painting, the features and forms that claim to reach the visible. The painter records, he does not invent. When El Greco or Caravaggio represent [*figurent*] an outline or sketch a face, of course they do not reproduce any outline, any face previously available in the field of the visible. Nor do they invent anything arbitrarily. They content themselves with recording the trace that imposes the unseen, from its own force. The traces that they pinpoint and let come up to the level of visibility by their own instinct do not follow any previously tracked groove. The lines and shapes mark the traces that have never before been sketched, traces of what has never before passed there, visible traces, not of an anterior visible but of the unseen as such—traces of the invisible. The painting opens the stigmata of the unseen: like scars, half-healed wounds of fractures imposed upon the neutral screen of the visible again virgin, not according to external or preexisting models, but by the obscure game of forces that gives birth to the unseen. Like the surface of the earth, which is fractured and folded under the pressure of invisible earthly [*telluriques*] forces, the magma of the unseen seeps out from the folds that, from the inside, take shape in the frame of the painting, rising to its surface like the fossils deposited by a torrent of lava. The painter, by his sensitive hand and quasi-volcanology, follows with a flowing brush—the most trembling one, that is to say, the most sensitive that it can be—the radically unforeseen trait that imposes itself. Just as the source under the "witching rod" [divining stick] vibrates contrary to every prediction and against every expectation—the painter senses the sudden appearance of a visible to which it would be irreligious for him to assign a reason, a cause, or a motive: to paint, this is always to paint *against* motive [*le motif*] and not *on the basis of* motive. Seismographer of the unseen, the brush records—far from imposing—the cracks of the unseen, such that they disrupt the already visible and, pushing it back, take up space like so many new visibles. In the painting, and in proportion to the faithful and persistent sensitivity of the painter, are inscribed from themselves the stigmata of the unseen. We may call them ectypes.[10] By ectypes, we are by no means speaking of types—impressions imposed from the outside by the spectator or worker [*l'ouvrier*]—but rather speaking of internal impressions, rising from the background [*fond*] of the painting; rising from the background of the painting, they thus suddenly appear in fact from the outside with respect to the spectator and the worker—external impressions, ambassadors of the outside of the gaze, and so on—types in the proper sense. Through these ectypes, the painting suddenly appears on its own terms [*à partir de lui-même*], traces its own path without following in the tracks of anything other than its own earthly, Dionysian [*telluriques*] movements. Self-stigmatized, it blazes its own trail, obedient to its organizing folds. This all happens as if the picture traced itself on its own terms: symbol only of itself; autonomous norm in the visible.

VII

The painting traces itself from itself by suddenly appearing in these ectypes. But the ectypes only mark the final accomplishment of this sudden appearance. They are thus not able, as it were, to burst to the surface of the visible in climbing back up from the unseen. So how to mark, in the painting nevertheless essentially visible, the original unseen? The unseen, as such and by definition, cannot be seen, but the painting cannot remain totally untouched by that from which it escaped. Between the strictly unseen and the purely visible ectype, like an airlock between its two incompatible states, at the background of the painting, behind the ectypes (from the point of view of a spectator), but before them (according to the odyssey of the sudden appearance), remains the bottom [*fond*] itself.[11] The background [*fond*] does not come afterward to surround or fill figures already visible by themselves; it points to the kingdom of the strictly unseen, like a border already seen from afar by one who has just crossed it and been liberated from it; the background is the unseen seen from the point of view of the visible, that from which the ectype has just extracted itself, the abyss that henceforth functions as a halo of light that comes to it from elsewhere; the unseen is overcome by the visibility that commences with an imperceptible invasion. The background is not added to the ectypes; rather the ectypes originate as from their most intimate unseen and, henceforth, the most foreign. The background of a painting of El Greco—for example in *Laocoön* or *View of Toledo* (which are in fact basically the same)—gives nothing to be seen, apart from the quasi-unseen, tormented and blurred already by the flood of the radiant visibility that the ectypes have just conquered coming back on this unseen—an inverted glory that humiliates the unseen and the vanquished by its generosity alone. The background, here, shows nothing: it testifies that it is from the background of the unshowable itself that the ectypes suddenly appear, miraculous survivors from the unseen. The background in *View of Toledo* shows nothing, above all nothing of the city of Toledo; it only marks the sudden appearance of what has become visible, of the group of the Assumption of the Virgin; it testifies, half-visible and involuntarily so, to what draws out the assumption and confirms that it is only a matter of an assumption: the passage into glory, the extraction from the darkness of the unseen. The background neither shows nor represents anything, except of course the enslavement of the unseen, called to the triumph of ectypes, witness to a counter-employment of the glory that it had claimed to repudiate. The assumption of the Virgin really accomplishes the assumption of the visible because these ectypes triumph over the unseen by escaping from the background.

The background [*le fond*] therefore must be understood as a fund [*un fonds*] (*fundus*, more fundamental, a hidden or subterranean reserve). From the reserve of the unseen (just as when the reserves of a museum restore to visibility a painting provisionally banned from view for a time, which is nevertheless restored by right), the ectypes suddenly appear. The fund here should be thought in terms of Aristotelian *physis*: at once the reserve that steals from visibility (according to the adage of Heraclitus, fragment 93)[12] but also that which climbs toward the desired form. The ectype suddenly appears from the unseen in the visible, but the unseen still shows through in the background [*le fond*] of the painting understood as its fund [*fonds*]. A fund—neither fundamental nor original, since the unseen abandons it and renounces it. A fund—at once paternal ground and murderer, a saturnine epistle that is denied, renounced, outstripped, and abandoned without remorse, for a gratuitous election to the visible, for a filiation—royal and by adoption—which annuls the natural filiation that had condemned it to the unseen. The ectype, this miracle of the visible, is resurrected from the heart of this fund [*du fond du fonds*].

Is it a matter, in this gap, of perspective? Certainly, in at least one sense, since the painting is deepened by an essential depth, according to which the gradations of the visible are organized: by being slackened in itself, the canvas becomes its own enemy and, in this same tension, understands by what an outpouring it is crossed—the arrow from the visible crosses the unseen, the arrow from a vault of the visible is resistant to the pressure of the unseen. But it is a matter of an inverted perspective, a counter-perspective, which is no longer organized in terms of the external gaze of the spectator, but rather prescribed in terms of the fund [*à partir du fonds*] under the direction of the ectype, as if the painting climbed back up from the unseen under the direction of the spectator, object and objective of perspective, no longer its author. It is the canvas itself that braces itself on its fund [*fonds*] in order to appear, that is only born to assert itself, to stretch itself—at once the arrow, string, and bow—toward the glory of showing itself, so that the fund, under this tension, erupts and lets the ectypes cross the border from the unseen to the visible. It is no longer a matter of inscribing upon a neutral surface, harmless and available, a complex of foreseen objects, because organized according to the subjective laws of intentional or synthetic imagination. It is a matter of representing the dark opening from which the unseen nevertheless expels the unforeseen [*l'imprévu*], to the great horror of the gaze, in a crushing defeat of the unseen as much as the foreseen—the eruption of the ectypes to the surface surprises, overwhelms, and subverts the painting, which, like us, expected everything except *this.* The vanishing point is found not in the background [*fond*]—in the fund [*fonds*]—of the painting but on the surface, or rather in our gaze itself. In effect, it might be more accurate to say that it is our gaze that can vanish before the unrestrained, dangerous torrent of ectypes, wild and orgiastic, thrown into a frenzy by the pleasure, even orgasm, of their appearance. The canvas yields, like the fund of the unseen from which it originates, under the assault of the ectypes. The painting offers to our terrified eyes the spectacle of a wall of the unseen, which cracks under the same pressure of the desire to appear. The flood of the visible overcomes it.

VIII

What commerce, what battle thus produces the painting? It is certainly necessary to resolutely renounce the reduction to a πόλεμος [struggle] between ὕλη [matter] and form, since here form clashes with the fund more than it informs it, but the gaze no more commands visibility than it pathetically endures its unforeseen initiative. Besides, more radically, the painting does not give forms to be seen. The spirit of forms, their invention like their almost mechanical inventory, can certainly give us a framework to demarcate the shipwreck—itself spectacular, inevitable, and without a doubt salutary—of contemporary painting (I mean since David and Ingres)—insofar as the painting does not have as its objective the production of forms, as delicious or disgusting as they may be. This objective is always concerned with objectivity, thus the essence of technique, which is to say, nihilism. As such, the painter does not have to produce forms. He must record, by a second and difficult passivity (the art of *doing* nothing), the eruption of ectypes from their fund, the rising of the unseen to the point of appearance. That to which the painting almost passively testifies consists—and thus immediately it is not subject to any consistency—in the distance between the fund and the ectype. A distance traversed from the unseen to the visible by the ectype, a distance traversed conversely from the visible to the unseen by the gaze. We by no means see there a peaceful synthesis, which governs and awaits all the remaining habitual objects, but rather the irreducible conflict where the unseen and the visible, the fund and the ectype meet only in order to confront one another and separate themselves.

The life of an authentic painting, a life by which it definitely excepts itself from the ancillary status of being an object, is due to the impossibility of identifying it with a simple region of the visible: it escapes this reduction by incessantly vibrating with the battle between the ectypes and the fund within it; the distance that it crosses straight through inflicts upon it a trembling, a setting under pressure, an elemental metamorphosis. The vagueness [*flou*] trembles with the painting that confronts the gaze, both stealing and provoking at the same time, not having awaited the stupid little virtuosities of *optic art*, the anamorphosis or the *trompe l'oeil* to exercise itself; or rather these could not be put into play if the painting, in its essence, did not always already contradict the expectation of the gaze, or at least only satisfy it by still frustrating it by the obvious fact of its own irreducibility to mere pleasantry or a flat equipmentality [*ustensilité*]. The painting lives off the distance itself where the ectypes and the fund confront one another with neither hatred nor reconciliation. It lives off their distance, because it breathes [*respire*] in it; it breathes (in) the distance, because this airing out [*l'aère*], rustling in it, there hollows out a cavern where it circulates. In the space of objectivity thus dug and renewed, the painting inhales and exhales. A grace raises it and in turn deposes it. Far from remaining inert under the watch of the gaze, the painting imposes its internal rhythm upon the spectator, who must follow it and adapt to it—as a dancer follows the rhythm of a musical piece. The distance, which airs out the painting, silently calls [it] to come and devote itself to the oscillations between ectypes and the fund. The gaze must thus cross the distance from which the painting draws its own life. It is the painting that brings the gaze to life, not the other way around. It is the painting that grants to the gaze the ability to make this crossing, as well as the climb from the unseen toward the visible, the liberation of the ectypes, and the exhausted collapse of the fund. Strictly speaking, it's not so much that we learn to see the painting as that the painting, by having given itself, teaches us to see it.

The serious game of painting is clearly brought out into the open here: first, the painting, perhaps before other still more unpredictable events, exposes us to the vision of what does not at all rise to the level of objectivity. So daily do we see innumerable visibles without, however, allowing them to stop us any longer than utility and desire require; we see only simple foreseen visibles, otherwise called objects, available because produced and managed. The painting, on the other hand, because it breathes in the distance between the unseen and the visible before presenting a new visible (and sometimes without presenting anything), hides every object from the gaze, or better, delivers the gaze from the objective restraints of an object. The painting confronts us with a nonobject, unavailable, unmanageable, unable to be (re)produced, unable to be mastered. A nonobject admittedly, a counter-object and not a simple antiobject, where the successive destruction of all the dimensions of the pictorial object reinforces by right the rule of objectivity, as its horizon remains intact. The painting, crossed and sustained by the irreconcilable distance between the fund and the ectypes, challenges every object and thus liberates our gaze from objectivity. The fact that the art market does not cease to claim to reinstate the painting into a context of objectivity (production, evaluation, economy, duplication, etc.) in no way contradicts this radical antagonism: it may be that the market succeeds in its ends, but in that way it will deal with nothing more than objects destitute of their own visibility from the unseen; it may be, to the contrary, that the assaults exasperate themselves so much more that they well up in vain against such a visibility that has suddenly appeared from the unseen. In a nihilistic context more than any other, the painting becomes for us one of the rare but powerful challenges to mastery. To learn from a painting to see a nonobject neither belongs to "aesthetics" nor is limited to that, but rather it concerns the purification of the gaze as such. There is still more: the painting does not train the gaze by conducting it to its ultimate possibilities insofar as it offers to it, beyond every opposing object, what phenomenology holds for the phenomenon par excellence—that it shows itself on its own terms [*se montre soi-même à partir de soi-même*]. The painting does not live in a peripheral section of the phenomenal universe, rendered secondary by some function of imitation; it appears by right in the region of privilege reserved for phenomena par excellence—those that appear in terms of their own proper distance, out of the confrontation within them between the unseen and the visible. The painting does not amuse or entertain, does not decorate or embellish, and shows nothing—it shows itself, from itself and for itself. And thus, in this self-showing on its own terms alone, it shows us above all what this is—to show itself, to appear in full authority, full glory, like the dawn of a new world. In other words, "To give the image of what we see, by forgetting all that has appeared before us."[13]

IX

Here then is the painting, nude. It does not offer any object to be seen, but breathes in the distance within it between the ectypes and the fund. Thus it transmits to our gaze its own movement as the imprescriptible condition to be able, precisely, to follow with one's eyes the ascent of the unseen in it to the visible. Strictly speaking, the painting offers nothing—no object, no thing, nothing other than itself—to the gaze, to be kept under a fixed eye.

And yet what do we see in and with this *irregardable*?[14] The invisible distance between the visible and the unseen, the fund and the ectypes. But *this* invisible, even if the painting does not cease to give it, is given to our eye insofar as it is *welcomed.* This is the paradox of the painting (but not of it alone): that the more its own evidence increases, the more its reception depends on the possibly myopic gaze of its spectator (who is squinting, to say the least). The painting imposes its reception like an ordeal [*une épreuve*] of sight, which discovers there the limits of its ability to see. But the painting also imposes upon itself the ordeal of subjecting itself to the doubtful reception of a possibly inept gaze. This double ordeal plays itself out in a unique act: vision as reception of a gift made to eyes that did not expect it. To see is to receive, since to appear is to give (itself) to be seen. This strikes us as similar to the common expression "to see what gives [*voir ce que cela donne*]."[15]

"To see what gives" means first of all: to stand back in order to better envisage the result of a stroke or a sketch that one has just inscribed upon the canvas. But this stepping back indicates above all that the one who has just physically put the color or lines on the surface of the canvas did not know, at the moment of effecting it, what he did, since, in order to see its effect, he must detach himself from his work, in order to learn, afterward, what visible appears there. He thus admits that, despite all his work, it is not he who put in the work on the painting but the painting itself, which, thus humbly called to appear upon the occasion of the work, opens itself to the visible on its own initiative. In order to see what gives, it is thus necessary first to admit that this [que cela]—the painting—gives *itself* [*se* donne], and the pictorial act is restricted to a matter of welcome, recording and being undergirded by the support of a gift. To paint means: to await a donation.[16] Further, in order to see *what* gives—that is to say, that which gives even that which is given—it acknowledges being made possible on the basis of donation. Being made possible on the basis of donation means surrendering itself to it and according to the measure by which it demands to be received. Every authentic painting attempts, by means of labor, not to produce some visible that must be, but to erect the verbal process of what was given to it—pulled out from the unseen. And just as the gift surpasses the scope of the welcome, the painter must be stretched, by means of labor and working on oneself (and not, at least at first, on the materials of visibility), in proportion to what comes to him, which is often disproportionate to the measure of expectation.

The visible gives itself to be seen. It is not yet a matter of revelation, but it is already a matter of what will possibly [*éventuellement*], perhaps later, have to bear the weight of glory inflicted by a revelation, which is always possible (for the worst always remains possible, and, for a gaze, such a revelation would indeed impose the worst possible experience, where its death would be a possibility, even a necessity). Thus with a mere painting, it is still not a matter of receiving a revelation; but in the face of the unforeseeable [*l'imprévisible*], it already admits without any doubt the greatest secret of the unseen—the fact that it gives itself. The visible always gives itself to the unforeseen [*l'imprévu*], as the unforeseen. It appears as the unforeseen because it gives itself, by itself, and on the basis of itself [*du fonds de lui-même*]. And yet every donation demands that one receive it. Before even the least of paintings, it is thus necessary to avert one's eyes, in order to venerate what gives itself there. Only then can we raise them, with a slow respect, to that One that gives what is given [*ce que donne ce qui se donne*].[17] And then finally to wait to see what gives.

3

The Blind at Shiloh

I

The liberation of the image—how much we required it, provoked it! And the image, in the end, has already been liberated. What we want, we have irrevocably. As free, it is neither censored nor technologically limited. Being free, it infiltrates, besieges, reigns. We recognized it before all the virtues: in principle it informs, teaches, entertains, gathers people together: in short, it contributes to liberty, equality, fraternity. In the end, the plastic arts are able to encounter "life," since they no longer consist in images as such. Knowledge is opened at last to the public, since henceforth the image assures its advertisement. The sacred no longer hides itself, since—far from disappearing—it appears in these "High Masses" that, as one says, are found henceforth more often in political congresses or athletic encounters than in eucharistic celebrations. In the end, desire drags its objects out from obscurity, since it is nothing more than an image that can be made visible and thus, in one sense, acceptable, or at least accepted in the circuit of distribution. The image becomes for us more than a mode—[it becomes] a world [*une mode—un monde*]. The world is made into an image [*s'est fait image*]. To speak a platitude, we live in the audiovisual epoch of history—and with every expectation of a long life, a virtual thousand-year reign.

It would be fitting therefore to celebrate this tranquil revolution with fervor and without reticence. However, we will not participate. We will not say that the audiovisual revolution neither liberates nor reveals. For it is necessary—if there is still room in the midst of the soft *consensus* that stifles us already—to pose a simple question: As the image of what does this image offer itself? In other words: from which original does the image originate? To what original does it return in the end? Here, the response is obvious. Any journalist, television producer, indeed television viewer will reply with sufficiency and commiseration: the image has no other original than itself and itself alone. In fact, the necessity of postulating that an image referred to any original would be taken to be largely due to an anachronistic lack of culture and concealed metaphysical obscurity; it is precisely the image released by contemporary technique that liberates itself as such because it frees itself—finally!—from the requirement of an original other than itself that would govern it. Today, the image covers the surface of the earth—in addition to the surface of the eyeballs [*des globes oculaires*] of the inhabitants of the world—only insofar as it produces itself, multiplies itself, and expands without restriction or reference. In the case of [economic] inflation, the monetary mass can grow without any restriction imposed by gold reserves or exchange; here the visual mass grows so much better because it is never commanded by any original; this is not to say that what one shows defines precisely the condition of the monstration. But the image, in contrast to paper currency, accrues [*accroît*][1] its authority by disconnecting itself from every original: the less gold there is, the more value the image has; so the dollar is not an image; but fortunately, the images produce dollars. In short, the liberation of the image consists precisely in its being liberated from every original; the image is valued in itself and for itself, because it is valued by itself. The image has no original other than itself and undertakes to make itself acceptable only to the unique original.

II

The arrogance of the image is marked most notably by its televisual development, insofar as the television is valued as a universal mode of being that overflows even onto images not directly produced by electronic equipment. The television is not limited to pursuing, by other means, what cinema—and before it, theater—have already accomplished. These always, at the very same moment that they produce fiction, maintain a relationship between the image and the original. Theater [does so], of course, because the original remains present at the same moment where, with my active consent, the illusions are born from images from another world: I will applaud, in terms of the representation of images, the original in the flesh and in person, acting here and now. Film certainly hinders or even prohibits this return to the ideal: the actors were able to die, flee, and hide themselves, disappearing into anonymity; but, by right, I can find them at a film festival, or better, attend a film shoot (for this film or the next), indeed learn in the books who the actors were. In short, even in the most deliberate fiction, the image at least refers back to a reality—in this case, the actors. A fortiori so was it the case with the "Actualité Pathé" of ancient times: I did not have to succumb to the harangue of a promoter to know that this image, even when deformed by propaganda, had "something of truth" about it. This refers back to an original that the televisual image destroyed.

Before delivering [*livrer*] to us the image of any original, television liberates [*délivre*] images—widows of every intentionality. First because, in the televisual order, the principal caesura between the image (as avowed fiction) and reality has disappeared: the *time* of representation. Every screening or performance used to admit a limit, precisely the duration of the performance of irreality. But television abolishes this time; there is neither a first nor a last showing: without interruption the electron gun bombards the screen and there reconstitutes the images, day and night, around the clock ("The channel that never sleeps"). The unending flow of time—a mark of the actuality of the real world in philosophy—here becomes, on the contrary, a constitutive trait of imaginary fiction. The irreality thus competes with the temporality of reality: as soon as its programs openly aspired to coverage twenty-four hours a day, seven days of the week, television confessed its essential goal: to appropriate the actuality of the world while reproducing it—or better, while directly *producing* it. The images, like manufactured objects, depend upon a production, a "production company." The lack of distinction between the world and the flux of images inscribes itself not only in the televisual use of time but also in the televisual use of *space*. This can be seen all the more in an example that would seem to contradict the preceding thesis: television news, news reports, and so on. Here, without manipulation or censorship, the image indeed refers to this or that actual event, from the most real world; certainly, but the images make available to the gaze events not only without common measure, without connection of meaning between them, but above all from geographic origins so dispersed, sometimes so heterogeneous, that we have at our disposal not a single imaginable world, lived and familiar, to welcome them, organize them, in short, to comprehend them. The space that these images throw into my face—whether geographically far or near is of little import—I cannot claim to attain there myself, not only because I lack equipment but because it has no place in the world in which I in fact live. The space that instantaneously crosses the televisual flow of images gives not a single possible world but rather discord—a blur. Thus space and time no longer constitute the a priori structures of experience but instead constitute the a priori conditions of the impossibility of any real experience—of the impossibility of moving back from images to their conditional [*éventuel*] original. Paradoxically, a television news report shows me nothing that I would know thanks to it; on the contrary, it enumerates for me all that I will never be able to know, since the original, in manifestly appearing for me, is lost at that moment. The televisual image does not have the time to move across the space that separates it from its original—of which, in fact, it should have the honesty to acknowledge it is the *forclusion*.[2]

The image, closed off to its original, thus no longer has any reality other than itself. This reality [*réalité*] finds its only reality or actuality [*effectivité*] on the televisual screen. The image produces itself on the screen because, being a screen[3] to its original, it produces itself only by becoming identical to its support, the screen. It is admirable that one then calls the screen the place of the image—since one then implicitly recognizes that an image cannot deploy itself (escape) as such while being on screen. To what, except to the original? The image produces a screen only because it is the screen that produces the image—in the place of the original. The screen—and thus the electronic cannon—produce the image in the place of reception [of welcome, *la recevoir*] (like the cinematographic screen). It produces the image according to an uninterrupted time and by covering an unlimited space that imitates that of the world, nevertheless without belonging to the world. The screen, this antiworld in the world, produces images without ever referring them to some original: form without matter, the image maintains only a ghostly reality, completely spiritualized. Admittedly, it could still be said that such an image refers itself to an original—but, as its spectator, I will never know it; between the fictive image and the image without original, the distinction escapes me. Fiction and special effects belong to a normal regime of the image on the televisual screen, the reference to an original being the exception.

On the basis of what criteria could such an image be governed? Since the original for it is lacking, it is thus governed by the one who sees it. Like every object, it settles on the subject, active or passive, who constitutes it on the basis of the simple fact of being able to welcome it and support it by the gaze. And *de facto* the televisual image is measured to the viewer [*le voyeur*]. Completely contrary to the view (which, to it, sees the unavailable and invisible), the viewer devours the visible that is all the more available. A "viewer": thus is defined the one who, under the most neutral names of "spectator" or "consumer," undergoes, governs, and defines the image—all under the pretexts of access to information, the opening of the world, and "connecting" on (albeit poor) coverage of current events of situations even more trivial and yet more restrictive.

The viewer watches for the sole pleasure of seeing: thanks to technology, he is finally able to succumb without limit or restriction to the fascination of the *libido vivendi*, which was always denounced by the Fathers:[4] a pleasure [*jouissance*] of seeing, of seeing all, especially what I do not have the right or strength to see; the pleasure also of seeing without being seen—that is, of mastering by the view [*vue*] what does not return to me without exposing me to the gaze of another. The viewer thus maintains a perverse and impotent relationship with the world that it both flees and possesses at one and the same time in the image.

The viewer fixes the norm of the image without original by the demand of his desire to see merely in order to see; each image thus becomes valid, so long as and as soon as it satisfies this desire, filling it perfectly or partially; thus the image must be conformed to the expectation of this desire. Whence the efforts of announcers, programmers, producers to target this desire, to measure it in order to satisfy it. But these pompous "communication strategies" themselves rest upon an implacable principle: every emitted image, in order to be seen by its viewer, must precisely satisfy his desire to see, its limits and its demands; thus every image must reproduce in itself the measure of a desire; this is to say that every image must make itself the idol of its viewer. With the image, the viewer sees the satisfaction of his desire, thus of himself. Every image is an idol, or it isn't even seen.

The image, joyously widowed by its original, accomplishes not a single element of liberation, nor does it open up a single new perspective: it only confirms a determined metaphysical situation—nihilism. If one admits that metaphysics, from its Platonic origin, established the opposition between the thing itself and the image in favor of the thing and, at its Nietzschean phase, reversed this opposition in favor of the image, taking it to be as real as the thing itself, then it is necessary to say that the idol of the viewer simply and precisely satisfies the demands of nihilism: nothing in itself, everything is according to the measure of the evaluation that ratifies it, or not. The televisual idol appears only if the viewers value it—the poll, in its derisory tyranny, illustrates in the mode of the ridiculous the revaluation of all the values by the superman (that is to say, the petty telespectator). The viewer, who values his idol, satisfies absolutely the metaphysical principle: *to be is to be perceived.*

III

As soon as the image has lost access to an original, it becomes an original itself—immediately and inevitably—under the mode of a pseudo- or counter-original. To become an image, "to go on the air," defines the mode of presence par excellence and no longer its merely derivative mode. An event does not prove its reality by having indeed taken place; for if it takes place, it takes place only in a determinate time and place, with actors and spectators in a limited number, in short in a world that is defined since it is real. And yet the real world has disappeared, since the image there makes a screen of its counter-world; henceforth, to have actually taken place, the event must be produced in the counter-world itself—it must reduce itself (or "pull itself up," it matters little) to the level of an image. Only this counter-world frees itself from the limits of space and time, and diffuses the event without end, in the dull irreality of the dream. Thus, it is better to appear than to be, since to be is not to appear. Better a minuscule manifestation on a grand plane than an immense manifestation on a reduced plane; better a well-"covered" silliness than an ignored performance. The technological possibility of being seen by an indefinite mass of viewers gives, today, a despotic power to the trivial (and Sartrean) adage: "I am what the look of others wants (and sees) that I should be." The necessity—to which even the best (above all) succumb—to show oneself, to make oneself seen, not to pass unnoticed, rests on a metaphysical principle: *to be is to be perceived.* Following a strict reversal of Platonism, we admit that the image *is* as much as—indeed more than—the thing itself: what I *am* does not remain behind what I appear to be; on the contrary, what I appear to be (the *look*)[5] invests my identity bit by bit and, in the end, completely, the deep strata of the person. To maintain one's identity is to recognize and at the same time to transmit an image of oneself, a self-as-image [*un moi-comme-image*]—which should satisfy both the viewers and the view [*le vu*]. This desire for image—the desire to completely become an image—exhausts the entire wisdom of our time: even the sage is wise through his image; he is wise as an image. All wisdom, in every field, amounts to making oneself as wise as one's image. For politicians, athletes, journalists, CEOs, writers, nothing is more precious than this—"my image": I am only a self-as-image.

Publicity. The term imposes itself here, beyond its current usage. By "publicity" we understand first of all the mode of being of every reality traced back to the status of an image: I am *because* I am seen, and *as* I am seen; what constitutes me is first and foremost the image that I become, always available for transmission, broadcast, and consumption by the viewers. But precisely when the image that I am returns or is iterated to the viewers, it falls in line with a second demand: so that myself-as-image can be returned to the viewers, it is necessary that they value it as suitable to them. Since the viewers judge myself-as-image as voters, supporters, readers, or fans, it must necessarily be that they recognize in myself-as-image the object that their desire expects, rather as an objectified image; it is thus necessary that myself-as-image delimit itself according to the exact expectations of their desire; now this desire finds only an idol, that is to say, the image of an image. I must constitute myself as an image, no longer first an image of me, but rather an image of the idol expected by the viewers—an idol, the image of a desire, thus of a voyeuristic gaze; I must, in order to be, give myself up, twice: to the gaze and to the desire of the viewers. My own desire to be seen demands, in the end, that I let myself be seen as an approximate image of the idol desired by those who, in order to be, see. The ambition to dominate, in whatever field it might be, paradoxically requires being reduced to the rank of an idol—thus an idol of viewers. From which we get the modern myth of *the big picture* [*le grand vu*]: the one that, as image, gives rise to and satisfies the desire of all the viewers: whether it be the cosmic actor (whose excesses the mass concerts mime), or the great communicator (who governs while making himself seen on the screen), or in the end, the great prostitute ("God," according to the definition risked by Baudelaire). Prostitution, taken in a strict sense: a face (in fact everything) attains being, under the regime of the televisual image, only insofar as it accepts not only being reduced to self-as-image [*soi-comme-image*] but above all conforming this first image to the draconian laws of another image—the idol (of desire) of the viewer. From which comes the illusion of expecting that an absolute reality will suddenly appear among the new images, a new original, finally adapted to the televisual regime of the visible: but images cannot deliver any original other than the same one that they know; the most beautiful image of the world can give only what it has—an original-in-image, a counter-world where the original remains always an image. To *be*, here, will only ever be to be *seen*. To be seen will only ever be to prostitute oneself, to mime the idol of the viewer. The great prostitute—Babylon—designates nothing less than a world, our own, which is a mode of presence, the televisual image. In order to be, it is necessary to be seen, thus to expose oneself as an image of an idol—the original immediately becomes inaccessible, since it appears as specter of itself. The original disappears, unless it makes itself an image—*to be is to be seen.*

The image takes the place of the original, since nothing *is* if it is not seen, or has just been seen, on the screen. Thus the original disappears either by remaining invisible or by being imagined (by becoming an image pure and simple). The broadcasting and production of images has as its goal not the opening of a world but rather the (en)closure of it by a screen; the screen substitutes for the things of the world an idol constantly repeated for viewers, an idol multiplied without spatial or temporal limits, in order to attain the cosmic scope of a counter-world. The televisual image, structurally idolatrous, obeys the viewer and produces only prostituted images. This onanism of the gaze fulfills the metaphysic of the monad: every supposed extroverted perception of the world is reduced to an expression of the monad itself, deploying its only essence in images taking the place of the world. The "communication" of images thus exerts a strategy for the consumption of visual goods and is obedient to the market needs of the viewers; far from being a disruption, it assumes the autistic monadism of the viewers. Such "communication" not only communicates nothing—other than images, idols of viewers, without original—but goes against all communion. The exchange of idolatries requires a screen before every gaze: I only ever look at the screen that imprisons me outside of the world. The screen closes me off from the world, the channels [*les chaînes*] chain me to the screen, the programs [*la grille*] lock me there all the time. The image constitutes every prototype into an idol, because it is itself first devalued to the level of an idol. Doubly retaining the possibility of referring back to an original, which it should be, the image tyrannizes the world, things, and souls. We know today, following the violence of weapons (war) and the violence of words (ideology), the terror of the idolatrous image; like the preceding ones, this violence bears a grudge against our souls—but, to reach there, it no longer exercises this blackmail upon our bodies (as in war) or upon our intelligence (as in ideology). It takes hold of our desire itself: the tyranny of the idolatrous image defeats us with our willing consent. We desire to see or be seen by only what is proportionate to our desire. Henceforth all can pass—through the screen; there on the screen is all to see and to communicate, but nothing to give or receive, since nothing persists outside the screen. The *libido vivendi*, which satisfies itself with the solitary pleasure of the screen, does away with love by forbidding sight of the other face—invisible and real.

IV

The *libido vivendi*, a pure desire to see that establishes a strict equivalence between the image and the thing, determines a world where everything is reduced to an image and where every image is valued as a thing. This equivalence is an absolute tyranny: the entry into the world of images does less to liberate the imaginary for a jubilant pleasure than it does to confine our spirit and our desire outside of things, as in a prison of images—an imaginal exile. The censure that the image (erected in a thing) exerts in our world no longer authorizes the least bit of access to the original, simply reducing it to the status of an unimaginable, an unimagable (that which cannot be imaged): what cannot be seen, simply is not. The original must therefore disappear, since, by definition, it can never appear.

This simple fact, however, deserves interrogation: does invisibility indicate, in the case of a possible original, the pure and simple denial [*dénégation*] of its reality? In other words, does the fact that the original remains invisible suffice to disqualify every possible original? Indeed, it could be that the original defines itself precisely by its very invisibility—by its irreducibility to its placement in an image. Let us consider three examples of such a principled invisibility. Admittedly, knowledge [*la connaissance*] always traffics in images, sensible or intelligible; in fact, to know a thing supposedly always consists in reconstituting it in terms of a series of images (and concepts)—a constitution that is in principle incomplete and undefined. I never *see* a cube: rather, along with the images of three of the sides, I constitute a "thing" that I will never see from a single glance (the six sides), but I give the six sides to it on the basis of the first three coupled with the requirements of the mathematical concept of the cube. In this perception, the referent or the thing itself remains invisible to me: I really see only certain aspects, certain parameters, in virtue of which I infer a totality that, really, I never have before my eyes. This gap between what is seen [*le vu*] and the original invisible can be described, in philosophical terms, as the difference between accidents (or attributes) and substance, between the phenomenon and the thing in itself, between fulfilling intuition and intention, between the sign and the referent, and so on. As a result, we live and we move not in the middle of what we see, but in a relation—through what we see to what we don't see. What we do not see can take two forms. On the one hand, that which we cannot see completely, but which can, by means of subsequent gazes, become entirely visible (the cube, this page, this fountain pen, that car traveling down the street, a room, etc.)—the potential visible, always invisible in actuality. On the other hand we have that which we see, but which could never be equal to what we are really aiming at: if we are looking to experience something of the sublime, pleasure, the beautiful, or love, what we aim at in this spectacle does not come down to either what we in fact see or what we are attempting to experience; it is precisely a matter of that which most radically exceeds our interiority and which, in itself [*pour cela même*], exceeds it. Here the invisible will remain forever such: the invisible is confirmed by the increase of the visible itself.

Thus let us move to the second manner by which the invisible indicates its irreducibility. If I see, not really in the mode of objectivity, not some inanimate object but rather a face—what do I really see? Certainly an outline, a look [*une allure*], a shape, the lines of the face, and so forth. But in the end these are not really important to me; this or that detail, this color, that grin can all change, without the face that I intend really varying to my eyes; one knows that a face can attract me (and strongly) to an insignificant character (insignificant to everyone other than to me) and that, conversely, I might never notice such evident characteristics of the beloved person (the color of the eyes, etc.). Is it a matter of a distraction or absent-mindedness? In no way, since my gaze, here possibly amorous, is intensely focused on this face, of which it wants to see everything, since it expects everything. But precisely, what it wants to see does not coincide with what this face gives to be seen to every other gaze; the indifference will see, without difficulty even amidst distraction, the color of the eyes or the details of the appearance; why therefore is it that I and my fascinated gaze do not see what the image of the other gives us so easily to see? Certainly because I do not want to see what is visibly given to be seen. What is it then that my gaze wants to see if not the visible of this face? Inevitably, it wants to see the invisible. But how could a visible face see what is invisible? How could a sensible gaze ever see something invisible? The response, which is paradoxical, goes nevertheless from oneself [*va pourtant de soi*]: my impassioned gaze can see, on the face of the other, only the sole place that does not offer anything to be seen—the pupils of the two eyes, obscure and empty holes. Why privilege this site that offers precisely nothing there to see? Because this invisible nothing signals not a single new visible, nor a counter-visible, but rather the invisible origin of the gaze of the other upon me. I see not the visible face of the other, an object still reducible to an image (as the social game and its makeup demands), but the invisible gaze that wells up through the obscurity of the pupils of the other's face; in short, I see the other of the visible face. Seriously (thus passionately) envisaging the face of the other comes down to intending there the invisible itself—that is to say, its invisible gaze placed upon me.[6] The intentionality of love thus exempts itself from the power of the image since my gaze, by definition invisible, claims to cross there another gaze, by definition invisible. Love escapes from the image, and that is why, when the image wants to take over love while visibly representing it, it sinks to pornography, meaninglessness, or a combination of the two.

There remains a third occurrence of the invisible. We have held that the gaze, beloved or loving, escapes the image and performs the invisible. But it is necessary to assume a final hypothesis: that this gaze could be holy to the point that, as a transparency, it could provide an icon of God, the invisible par excellence. This hypothesis is in fact offered in the case of Christ Jesus, whom Saint Paul does not hesitate to call the "icon of the invisible God" (Colossians 1:15).[7] How is this invisibility exerted here? Christ offers to the gaze only an icon, while showing a face, that is to say, a gaze, itself invisible. It is thus a matter, in a first instance, of a crossing of gazes [*une croisée des regards*], conforming to the schema in love; I look, with my invisible gaze, upon a gaze that envisages me; in the icon, in effect, it is a matter not so much of seeing a spectacle as of seeing another gaze that sustains mine, confronts it, and eventually overwhelms it.[8] But Christ does not offer only himself to my gaze to see and be seen; if he requires of me a love, it is a love not for him but for his Father; if he demands that I lift my eyes to him, this not at all so that I see him, him only, but so that I might see also and especially the Father: "Philip, he who has seen me has seen the Father" (John 14:9). But since the Father remains invisible, how can I see the Father when seeing Christ? Does not Christ constitute only what can be seen of the Father in place of the Father? On that interpretation, Christ would thus not show the Father but would be a substitute for him, a visible lieutenant of an invisible, which he would conceal by the very fact that he would claim to show it.[9] But Christ Jesus came to earth only to glorify the Father and in no way to draw attention to his own glory: "What shall I say, 'Father, save me from this hour?' But I came for this very hour. Father, glorify your name"

(John 12:27). We thus come to understand how Christ Jesus offers not only a visible image of the Father who remains invisible but even a (visible) face of the invisible itself (the Father), a visible image of the invisible *as invisible.* If one tried to evade this paradox, it would no longer be interpreted according to the logic of the image: if every image offered of the invisible God is a caricatural usurpation, it would be necessary therefore to condemn Jesus Christ to death for blasphemy, which is exactly what happened (Matthew 26:66). The paradox of an iconic monstration of the invisible in the visible would allow only the reception of Christ, without the crucifixion for blasphemy. But this paradox becomes intelligible only if we can release the icon from the logic of the image—and thus only if we ourselves can escape from the tyranny of the image. The invisible—of the thing, of the gaze, and of the "invisible God"—thus requires that we take a new plunge.

V

In the face of the contemporary situation of the image, which usurps every reality precisely because it sets itself up as the norm of every possible thing, we find a situation that appears to call for an attitude at once conceptually simple and spiritually holy: iconoclasm. If the image claims to establish itself as its own original, thus to be satisfied with itself, the invisible must claim invisibility, definitively. No face, especially not the one of the unique God, can either be seen or claim to be seen. To see God—that would be blasphemy, and in any case an impossibility. A number of religious movements have tended toward this radical response, not only in the seventh and eighth centuries, and not only in Islam or Judaism. One can even foresee that the response would win support in the future, only reinforcing the tyranny of the image under the pretext of resisting it. However, iconoclasm implies a complete rallying to this tyranny: in effect, it contents itself with merely inverting the common attitude in view of the reigning definition of the image as norm of the thing; instead of including there the face of God, iconoclasm confirms the divorce between this face and every image; by doing so, it completely legitimates the modern tyranny of the image as norm of the thing. And yet the seriousness of the debate demands examination, well beyond this development, to determine whether the modern (televisual) model of the image exhausts the essence of the visible, or whether perhaps it is possible to oppose it to a radically distinct model of the image. And could it perhaps be precisely the contemporary development of the image (in postcubist painting) that already sketches the elements of another image of image?

Historically at least, a model of the image has opposed itself to iconoclasm, and, at least in the Church, has won out. It is a matter of the icon. *Icon* does not designate a particular pictorial genre, for example "the icons" on wood (since Roman frescos and Byzantine mosaics or certain gothic statues are less icons than "the icons," and sometimes less than some others, belated and anecdotal). *Icon* here designates a doctrine concerning the visibility of the image, more exactly, concerning the usage of this visibility. This doctrine is characterized, in summary, by two radical innovations.

For the duo (or duel) of a spectator's gaze, objectively visible, it [the doctrine of the icon] substitutes a *third*: a spectator's gaze, objectively visible, but also a prototype. The prototype does not only play the role, at first here, finally very banal, of an original (mimetically reproduced by the objectively visible), of a referent (possibly inaccessible), or of a phantom from the nether world [*l'arrière-monde*]; it does not intervene as a second visible, behind the first, concealed by the first mimetic objectivity—uncontrollable, unusable, indefinitely repeatable; it intervenes as a second gaze that, as through the transpierced screen of the first visible (the painted or sculpted image, etc.), envisages the first visage, that of the gazing spectator. Before the profane image, I remain the viewer unseen by an image that is reduced to the rank of an object (the aesthetic object remains an object) constituted, at least in part, by my gaze. Before the icon, if I continue to look, I feel myself seen (I must feel myself thus in order for it to function effectively as an icon). Thus the image no longer creates a screen (or, as in the case of the idol, a mirror) since through it and under its features another gaze—invisible like all gazes—envisages me. The original thus does not belong to the objectivity (confiscated or not by the image) that it would reduplicate. The original intervenes, through the imaged objectivity, as a pure gaze crossing a gaze.

As a result, what is at stake in the operation of the icon concerns not the perception of the visible or the aesthetic but the intersection of two gazes; in order for the viewer to be allowed to see and escape from the status of being a mere voyeur, it is necessary for him to move, through the visible icon, toward the origin of another gaze, confessing and admitting to be seen by it. What the Second Council of Nicaea [787] formulated with the utmost precision is required: "For the more continually these [Christ, the Virgin, the saints] are observed by means of such representations[10] (δί εἰκονικῆς ἀνατυπώσεως ὁρῶνται), so much the more will the beholders be aroused to recollect the original [the prototype] (τῶν πρωτοτύπων), and desiring them and testifying to them; to these should be given respectful veneration (προσκύνησις), but not true adoration (λατρεία), which pertains only to the divine nature."[11] The "respectful veneration" is not to be confused with adoration: the one, in effect, is concerned with a (real) nature, the other a (irreal, intentional) gaze; before the icon, one should not adore, since the visible and real support (the image in its materiality) does not merit what a divine nature alone demands (in the Eucharist par excellence); but it is necessary to venerate, that is, by my gaze, to climb back up [*remonter*], to cross the visible image and be exposed to the invisible counter-gaze of the prototype. The icon is given not to be seen but to be venerated, because it thus offers its prototype to be seen. The icon is crossed by the veneration of my gaze in response to a first gaze. This is precisely what the Second Council of Nicaea decreed, taking up the felicitous formula of Saint Basil: "the honor paid to the icon is transferred [διαβαίνει, *transit*] to the prototype."[12] Thus the doctrine of the icon represents a radical break with the status of the image, since for the visible object (exclusive, today, of every other thing), it substitutes a visible transit where two gazes cross each other and are exposed to each other, viewers [*voyants*], the one seen, the other aimed at—at least.

It remains to determine which images can be qualified as icons. Since the icon is defined by a second gaze that envisages the first, the visible image is no longer a screen; on the contrary, it permits itself to be transpierced; but two gazes cross there. Thus the visible surface must, paradoxically, efface itself, or at least efface within it every opacity that would obfuscate the crossing of gazes [*la croisée des regards*]: the icon *dulls* the image in it, in order to there prevent any self-sufficiency, autonomy, or self-affirmation. The icon inverts the modern logic of the image: far from claiming its equivalence with the thing while flaunting itself in glory, instead it removes the prestige of the visible from its face, in order to effectively render it an imperceptible transparency, translucent for the counter-gaze. The icon does not expect one to see it, but rather gives itself so that one might see or permit oneself to see through it. A dulled, dressed-down image—in short, transpierced—the icon allows another gaze, which it gives to be seen, to suddenly appear through it. It withdraws from the invisible evidence that it nevertheless reveals. The question can henceforth be formulated as such: where to encounter, originarily, an image that effaces its own visibility in order to allow itself to be pierced by another gaze? The answer is obvious: the Servant of Yahweh literally allows himself to be disfigured (shedding [*perdre*][13] the visible splendor of his own visage) in order to do the will of God (which will appear only in his actions). The Servant sacrifices his visage—he allows the effacement of his "image": "the multitudes were astonished at the sight of him; his form, disfigured, lost all human likeness; his appearance so changed he no longer looked like a man" (Isaiah 52:14; cf. Psalms 22:7). By completely effacing the glory of his own image, to the point of obscuring even his humanity, the Servant allows nothing other than his actions to be seen: these result from obedience to the will of God and thus allow it to become manifest. "I shall declare your name to my brethren; in the midst of the assembly, I will praise you" (Psalms 22:22). The self-renunciation of the image itself—a condition of its transformation into an icon—is thus accomplished in the obedience of the one who sheds his face, renouncing his visibility in order to do the will of God. By this paradoxical glory, Christ displays the logic of the iconic image: "Then they spat on his face and beat him; and others struck him with the palms of their hands, saying, 'Prophesy to us, Christ! Who is the one who struck you?'" (Matthew 26:67–68). In fact, it is precisely at the moment that he loses his human appearance [*figure*] that Christ becomes the figure of the divine will: in him, it is no longer his human appearance [*figure*] that is imagined [*se figure*]; and shedding appearance, he gives shape [*donne figure*] to a holiness that would have remained invisible without the shrine [*écrin*] (not screen [*écran*]) of his body. When, on the face, it undoes the glory of every image, the body remains what, in obedience to the will of another, shows this other all the more: "You desired neither sacrifice nor offering, you formed a body for me. You required neither burnt offering nor sin offering, then I said, 'Here I come!' In the scroll of the book it is written of me, I delight to do your will" (Psalms 40:7–9 [6–8], LXX). By accomplishing in the movements of the body not his own will but that of God, Christ indicates not his own face but the trace of God. His disfigured appearance is thus given as a transparency, in order that we might regard there the gaze of God. The dulling of the image, which is accomplished in the disfiguration of Christ, delivers the first icon: the veil of Veronica wipes away not a visible image but the kenosis of every figure—the kenosis of the image, "the condition of a slave" (Philippians 2:7)—and allows the trace of the invisible to appear, which envisages us.

VI

The icon, therefore, is derived from the kenosis of the image. The first kenosis (that of the Word [John 1:14]) permits the first "icon of the invisible God" [Colossians 1:15]. And vice versa: Christ testifies to us that he offers an authentic icon of the Father (not a mere image of himself) by the kenosis of his own will given over to the Father. The self-affirmation of the image, like all others, yields only in front of an abandonment: it is precisely because the icon is not given for itself, but rather undoes its own prestige, that it perhaps demands veneration—veneration that it does not seize but rather lets pass through it to the invisible prototype. It remains to be seen how the theological paradigm of a kenosis of the image translates into aesthetic principles. We must limit ourselves here to proposing some evidence in support of the aesthetic pertinence of such a kenosis.

Contemporary painting already practices, in certain schools at least (minimalist art, *art povera*,[14] ready made, etc.), a systematic impoverishment of the spectacle offered to the gaze by the work; on the one hand, it may be a matter of a choice of very banal materials, or even vulgar ones (cardboard, plaster, wrapping paper, various scraps, etc.); on the other hand, it may be a matter of giving up the inventiveness of plastic art, in the reuse of prefabricated objects and shapes, even in duplications without innovation, to infinity.[15] Hence the appearance of the non–art objects that, in the museum, are disappointing from the viewpoint of the observer, forces him, with pleasure or not, to reconsider his relation of pleasure and of possession with respect to the visible object. The strategy of these aesthetic approaches is intended precisely to liberate the gaze from the image (the deception being suspended by the spectator), and also to liberate the image from the gaze (the visible nullity being concealed by the desire of the observer); in short, to dissociate the mutual closure of the gaze and the image by each other. Of course, there it is a matter of a recognition of tendencies rather than a doctrine; without a doubt also, the impoverishment of the image does not take place, in the contemporary schools, until a second gaze envisaging the first is recognized through the screen of the visible; nonetheless, the fact remains that a strategy of the impoverished image effectively attempts to give to the gaze its free initiative and its problematic liberty.

One might wonder if Christian art was not attempting, consciously or not, in each of its genuine epochs, the practice of a kenosis of the image; unless it is on the contrary respect for this kenosis that is ordained (or not) by Christ. That not a single image claims self-sufficiency, but rather returns itself to an Other—this can be accomplished in a number of ways: either by digging the visible screen from a counter-gaze found to be invisible (as in "the icons," Roman and Gothic sculpture); or by diverting light, outside of its function of illuminating the present, toward the summons of the Infinite, of the invisible, of the unattainable (as in Baroque domes, Rubens, etc.); or by employing shadows and lights not to confirm the visible shapes but rather to confound and disrupt for the sake of the undecidable appearance of the invisible Spirit (Caravaggio, Rembrandt, Nain). More could be said about other, similar devices, but of particular importance is their common trait: that the prestige of the image or the visible object impoverishes itself [*s'appauvrisse*],[16] imposing limits on itself so that the veneration is brought back not to itself, the image, but rather to the prototype, possibly aimed at through it [*par lui éventuellement visable*].

If such poverty characterizes art insofar as it is Christian, one can draw a surprising but probable conclusion: the often indisputable meanness [*la laideur*][17] of art said to be "Sulpician" [*sulpicien*][18] ought not to be discredited. For as Andre Frossard remarked one day, in front of a *Virgin* by Raphael, "A Raphael!"; but in front of a Sulpician *Virgin,* one recognizes the Virgin herself. Thus Sulpician art practices, more than "great art," the impoverishment of the image and the transfer of veneration from the image to the original. Its unintentional *arte povera* assures that less than ever does it seize veneration for the sake of the image, thus protecting it against every tyranny of the image. This paradox of Sulpician art is obviously not sufficient to compensate for the obvious bankruptcy of religious art in the twentieth century; it explains why this is the case even less, seeing especially that the contribution of notable artists has done nothing to change this defeated situation. In their[19] chapels, it is simply a matter of recognizing, "That is by Matisse!," "That is by Cocteau!,"—thus, to see; but it is not a place of prayer—that is, of being seen; or better, it is necessary to forget [*oublier*][20] that these are "by Matisse" or "by Cocteau"—to forget the visible. These chapels celebrate their painters, not the addressee [the object of worship]—they play the role of simple idols, not of icons. If the lowly [*le laid*][21] does not offer to holiness its better shrine [*écrin*] (though does not holiness rid itself of every such treasure chest [*écrin*]?), the beautiful perhaps makes itself a screen [*écran*].

Where, then, is the paradigmatic kenosis of the image for the benefit of the holiness of God accomplished? In the liturgy. The liturgy proposes to demonstrate a visible spectacle, which summons and possibly fills vision, but also the senses of hearing, smell, touch, and even taste. It accomplishes an entire possible aesthetic and perhaps thus appears to be a complete spectacle, more than opera, which moreover is its mimic and, by the *oratio,* results from it. Nevertheless, this apotheosis of the image itself remains an illusion, or, by way of illusion, a deviation and a temptation. For, in the performance of the liturgy, the celebrant acts *in persona Christi*—in the name of Christ and as supporter of his role: Christ speaks in the readings, makes himself seen, touched, eaten, and breathed in his eucharistic body. Every liturgy effects the appearance of Christ and results from it. Of course it always remains possible to apprehend (in fact to miss) the celebration as a "grand mass," to know it as the ideological self-celebration and closed system of an Internet community, of a culture, or of power. But there it is a matter of a gaze already completely absorbed by the idolatrous spectacle and certainly closed to its crossing (or being crossed) by an invisible gaze. Whether one who sees the eucharistic liturgy as a spectacle is condemned less to idolatry than to himself, with regret or pleasure, is of little import. The attitude of my gaze before the liturgy determines my general attitude before the crossing of the visible by the invisible. It may be that only the liturgy summons us to such a decision: it provokes the last judgment of every gaze, which must, before it and it alone, either continue still to desire to see an idol or agree to pray. Prayer signifies here: letting the other (of the) gaze see me [*laisser l'autre (du) regard me voir*].[22] The liturgy alone impoverishes the image enough to wrest it from every spectacle, so that in this way might appear the splendor that the eyes can neither hope for nor bear, but a splendor that love—shed abroad in our hearts [Romans 5:5]—makes it possible to endure.

In order not to remain blind—obsessed by the incessant stream of static images that wall up [*murent*] our eyes on themselves—in order to be liberated from the muddy tyranny of the visible, one must pray—going to wash oneself in the pool of Shiloh.[23] At the pool of the Sent One, who was sent only for that—we are granted a vision of the invisible.

4

The Prototype and the Image

I

If, with respect to an image, it was a matter of demanding that it render visible the holiness of the Holy, would that not instead demand iconoclasm? For the holiness of the Holy par excellence is marked by being outside of every determination that would compromise its unconditionality or limit its infinity. The Holy, that protégé of immense separation, evades all comprehension, with respect to both mind and meaning. "Neither flesh, nor blood, nor human will" (John 1:13) is able to force into visibility "that which eye has not seen, nor ear has heard, nor has entered into the heart of man" (Isaiah 64:4=1 Corinthians 2:9), precisely because it is what "God has prepared for those who love him" (ibid.). But how can God himself prepare the invisible for visibility to every spectacle of its own glory? The iconoclastic [*iconomaque*][1] temptation does not cease to be revived and to seduce, in our own epoch more than any other certainly, because it obstinately reiterates an incontestable, though limited, fact: The Holy is never seen [*s'aperçoit*], since only the visible is seen, according to the measure of the sight granted to our reach. And yet every spectacle reaches visibility only by submitting itself to the conditions of possibility of objects of visual experience, that is to say an intuition, intelligible or sensible; in either case, the intuition itself is proportionate to the consciousness that receives it and is thus defined by finitude. On this principle, phenomenology and critical philosophy are agreed: no phenomenon enters into the visibility of a spectacle unless it first submits itself to the conditions of this visibility itself: the givenness [*donation*][2] to a finite consciousness. Consequently, the most basic piety should hold to this inevitable dilemma: either the Holy maintains itself as such, in which case it refuses itself to every visible spectacle, and the holiness of God remains without either image or visage; or the image that delivers the Holy to the visible simply abandons it as a victim to the torments of its executioners—and the image, widow of all holiness, fills the role of an obscene blasphemy. Either the invisible or the impostor. Retrieved in our time, the iconoclastic [*iconomaque*] alternative thus schematized gains a remarkable pertinence. We live—this is an indisputable platitude—in a world of images, where moreover the same flux of images perhaps strips us of a place in the world and an approach to the image. This situation reinforces the iconoclastic suspicion: among all these images—indefinitely renewed because absolutely vain, uniformly unseemly by virtue of their banality—what virgin space remains given to the possible visibility of holiness? Does not the imaginary torrent occupy every possibility, to the point of obfuscating, without the least remainder, the more modest reserve where the Holy can begin to appear, if only in the sketch of an enigma? Still further: If images, as today, no longer have only to submit to the conditions of possibility of experience but also still must be conformed to the conditions of the setting in spectacle [*la mise en spectacle*], should not the incompatibility between holiness and the lesser image provoke a fight to the death? The image, henceforth governed, beyond the conditions of its reception (intuition, finitude), by the conditions of its production (spectacle, message, diffusion), is directly and radically established as an idol—indeed, claims the title. And yet the idol constitutes only an invisible mirror delimited by the measure of the first visible that our gaze can aim at being filled by, thus the last visible that it can support without failing; the idol indirectly gives to be seen by the viewer's gaze the scope of his own gaze, by the mirror of an extreme spectacle; it closes itself to every other, because it shuts up the gaze in its finite origin. Only in such a world of images, thus of idols, could iconoclastic [*iconomaque*] violence appear as the unique defense against the universal blasphemy of spectacles—and first of all those that claim to exhibit in our visibility the glory of the Holy, which no one can see without dying.

II

The excess of the image did not characterize the epoch of the Second Council of Nicaea any more than our own, to be sure. Nevertheless this council delivered a theoretical decision for us, whose inspired audacity can enlighten us, even more than we, as historians, could enlighten ourselves. Understanding the Second Nicene Council demands, through but also beyond the hermeneutic labor of its text, that we interpret it for ourselves with the help of its fundamental concepts. These concepts are all ordered toward a decision: since the image, understood according to its usual logic, leads to an iconoclastic dilemma, the holiness of the Holy thus demands, in order that we receive there the revelation in visibility, that we construct a theoretical model absolutely other than that which leads to the idol—the model of the icon. Between the idol and the icon, the rupture tolerates not a single compromise. It remains to bring out how, phenomenologically, the icon escapes the catastrophic (iconoclastic [*iconomaques*]) consequences of the idol—that is, to elucidate in what way and within what limits Actio 7 of the Second Council of Nicaea opens up, for us also, an access of the invisible to the visible. The first decision is thus announced: "We define with all accuracy and rigor that, concerning a manner [of] approaching to the type of Cross (παραπλησί ως τῷ τύπῳ τοῦ . . . σταυροῦ) worthy of honor and invigoration, it is necessary to set up (ἀνατίθεσθαι, *proponere*) [for God] holy and respectable icons, [made] from colors, mosaics, and other suitable materials."[3] Icons are thus opposed to idols by two qualifications: first because they alone deserve and can demand the veneration of the faithful; second because they alone keep and manifest a trace of the brilliance of the holiness of the Holy. The second determination evidently guarantees the first: the icon can receive veneration only insofar as it visibly bears on its face the holiness of the Holy. The debate should thus first be concentrated, above all, on the mode of fidelity of the icon—which remains an aesthetic object, made from the explicitly mentioned materials—toward the glory of the Holy. What is this fidelity based upon? How is this fidelity founded? What are the criteria for determining this fidelity?

The canon[4] invokes a "manner [of] approaching," which it is not necessary (despite the emphasis of the Latin translation, *sicut . . . ita . . .*) to understand as a comparison, even less as a similarity [*similitude*]: παραπλησίως indicates approximation, the point of approach [*le fait de s'approcher de*], without either confusion or assimilation. Between which terms does the approximation play? Between the τύπος τοῦ σταροῦ, the mark of the Cross, on the one hand, and the icons on the other. One would thus understand, following the most neutral reading, that the worship of icons should be restored by being elevated approximately to the degree of dignity of the worship of the Cross. But this reading (besides the fact that ἀνατίθεσθαι can be translated as "restore" [*restaurer*] only with difficulty) ignores a fact that is essential, although in part concealed by the canon itself: On the one hand, the Cross is always called a type: τύπος τοῦ σταροῦ [a type of the cross], the council twice iterates.[5] On the other hand, the icon itself always receives the title of τύπος; if the canon does not explicitly confer it, it suggests it while quoting *in fine* what would become the normative principle of Saint Basil: "The honor given to the icon passes to its prototype, ἐπί τὸ πρωτότυπον":[6] in the face of a πρωτότυπον, the icon can barely appear as a τύπος. But above all, at least since John of Damascus, the icon should be understood, equally, as a τύπος: "The prototype, this is what is put in the icon (εἰκονιζόμενον), from [*à partir de*] what produced it. [Otherwise] by virtue of what did the people of Moses prostrate themselves around the tabernacle carrying the icon and the type (εἰκόνα καὶ τύπον) of what is in heaven?"[7] Very systematically, John of Damascus considers the relation of the icon to that which it shows according to the possibilities of the *typical* [*la typique*]: "icons are the visible [terms] of invisibles and nontypes, [henceforth] corporeally types (ἀτυπώτων συματιχῶς τυπουμένων) in order to permit a confused knowledge [*une connaissance confuse*]"; in short, icons are "the types of that which has no type, τύποι τῶν ἀτυπώτων."[8] The icon, like the Cross, is equivalent to a type. The canon [Actio 7] presupposes this equivalent status, precisely in order to ground the dignity of icons theologically: they should also be received as types, according to a mode that approaches the type par excellence: the Cross.

The approximation that renders the icon—as τύπος—of the Cross—as also τύπος—can moreover go as far as the interpretation of the sign of the Cross—the crucifix—directly as an icon. Thus John of Damascus risks the pure and simple assimilation of the two τύποι: "And indeed often, while we do not have the spirit of the sufferings of the Lord, by viewing the icon of the crucifixion (έικόνα τῆς σταυρώσεως) of Christ, these sufferings return to us in memory, and falling to our knees, we venerate what is set in the icon (τῶ είκονιζομένω), not the material of which it is made"; here, with the Cross as τύπος, it is very much a matter of venerating the έκτύπώμα made accessible by an icon. And he confirms the iconic status, thus typical status, of the Cross by adding that it has no need of any reproduction of its original: "For what difference does it make whether or not the Cross bears the έκτύπώμα of the Lord?"[9] Thus the conciliar declaration establishes a first point concerning the status of the icon: it holds the rank of τύπος, but this τύπος should itself be taken as an approximation of the first τύπος, that of the Cross where Christ died, such that the crucifix and all icons of the Cross render it accessible to us. The icon bears the glory of the Holy—"The icon is a triumph, as well as a manifestation"[10]—but it faithfully bears such by attesting only to a type, and really only the type of a type, *typus autem Crucis.* The first type is revealed, before the icon, in the Cross. The Cross indeed accomplishes first and perfectly the trait that distinguishes a type from, for example, an image: it does not reproduce its original according to degrees of similitude but rather refers itself paradoxically to a prototype more indicated than shown. The Cross does not offer any spectacle or image of Christ; it does not resemble it any more than it differs from it; simply, it should not be regarded according to any register of either similitude or dissimilitude. What it exhibits to everyone's gaze defers [*differe*] in such a way that it visibly speaks from itself; born as "the most beautiful of sons of men" (Psalms 45:2), he dies "a worm and not even a man" (Psalms 22:6), in such a way that "he no longer appeared human" (Isaiah 52:14). Christ, on the Cross, holds no more than a typical relation, outside of similitude or dissimilitude, with himself. Never the image as such, he is only more radically disqualified when the absolute Face—far from just letting his glory be completely submerged in the space of the visible in a permanent and unlimited transfiguration—submits to the violation not so much of his divine visage but more of his lesser human visage (for no one from among us would want, as visage, what men have given to Jesus). On the gallows of the Cross, nothing is more exhibited than the unnamable, than what cannot be named in any language (and that is why Pilate had to employ no fewer than three idioms to attempt to identify it). Christ kills the image on the Cross, because he crosses an abyss without measure between his appearance and his glory. He definitively disqualifies the least pretension of an image to produce or reproduce what it might of the glory of the original, and thus he fulfills—even within his Incarnation, by it and not despite it—the Old Testament prohibition: "You shall not make for yourself any idol (εἴδωλον), nor any likeness (ὁμοίωμα) of what is in heaven above or on the earth beneath or in the waters under the earth" (Exodus 20:4). Thus the τύπος του τιμιου και ζωοποιου σταυρου [type of the precious and life-giving cross] well deserves these qualifications; it testifies to its honor (τιμιος) by deposing in it every idolatry; it gives life (ζωοποιος) by liberating us.

But, by accomplishing the type par excellence, does not the Cross immediately prohibit every other type? And this for two reasons: the Cross gives a figure of Christ only under the paradox of a secret glory, thus a concealed visibility; further, the Cross, renouncing for itself any similitude, cannot be guaranteed, even "approximately," by similarity to other types, thus to other icons. Would not the interpretation of the Cross as the type par excellence lead to an iconoclastic [*iconomaque*] disqualification of every other image of Christ? Even more, would it not be fitting, since every τύπος refers back to a πρωτότυπον, to renounce, in addition to icons, even the Cross itself? This objection is strong only in appearance and, from the outset, it admits its weakness: it operates entirely within the horizon of similitude or a logic of *mimesis*, since it concludes from nonsimilitude to pure dissemblance, and from this dissemblance it concludes the illegitimacy of every image. And yet, every question that opens the type of the Cross (thus consequently other possible types) comes back to a demand: Is it possible for an image to remain bound under a ruled relation to a prototype without having to obey the laws and demands of the mimetic? And yet, in place of the mimetic, icons substitute an approximation (παραπλησίως) toward the prototype; in order to understand it, it is thus appropriate to see if and how the type par excellence—the Cross—relates to its possible prototype. For the icon only gives Christ to be seen in his holiness in the same way that the Cross gives to be seen—renders visible—the divine holiness of Christ. The question thus remains to be asked: Just what does the Cross actually give to be seen? Does it offer the type of a prototype?

This fitting together of two pieces of wood raised up as a gallows gives nothing as such to be seen of the least holiness or the least divinity—except a human body that one may have perhaps already seen before he had been put to death. As such, the Cross does not produce any new spectacle: neither the dying body nor the infamous crosspiece adds anything to the visible that was not available before. For the passersby and pilgrims going up to Jerusalem, the ones dying on the crosses probably offered—given the harshness of the time—only a spectacle that would have been, in the end, banal and common; the Roman soldiers would have dispersed the crowd with a simple "Keep it moving, there's nothing to see!" more truly still than the intention of "making an example." However, there were some spectators there, the ones cursing, the others lamenting; admittedly, but do these really constitute spectators? No, since in the face of the same sinister exhibition their comportments toward the state of affairs differs because, though they see the same visible, they do not discern the same evidence. Or rather, in the same visible, they recognize, on the basis of different marks, different meanings, which are equally invisible even though all informed and organized by this visible. The invisible meaning recognized by enemies and unbelievers construed it as the failure of a false Messiah; to the compassionate, it is the death of a just man abandoned by God as well as men; finally and above all, the invisible meaning recognized by the "centurion who was standing right in front of him," the dying Christ—this visible nonspectacle of a fleeing life—is "truly the Son of God" (Mark 15:39 = Matthew 27:54). The centurion saw (ἰδὼν) the same thing that everyone else saw—the same sinister yet visible spectacle. However, he alone recognized there the visible trace of the invisible God; he interpreted this corpse as a sign of God—or better, as the one who is God. The transition turns not on an illusion but on a hermeneutic of all vision, even the most profane and banal, already implied; it simply reaches a climax in this case, to the point of a paradox; indeed the distance between the invisible sense and effectively visible spectacle is never so ruptured as it is here, where it is a matter of crossing from this exhausted corpse to the glory of the living God. If, however, the centurion crosses any such abyss, it is because he grounds his interpretation on the Cross itself, or rather on its function as τύπος: it brings right into the visible the type and mark of the invisible; the corpse of Jesus bears the marks [*les stigmates*] of the living God. The invisible admittedly does not deliver itself in a visible spectacle to everyone, directly and without the mediation of a hermeneutic, but it does give itself to be recognized through a certain visible, which it invests overabundantly and as the sign of its mark without remainder. In order to contemplate Christ as such—as Son of the Father—it is never enough, neither before nor after nor during the Cross, [merely] to see Jesus of Nazareth;[11] it is always necessary to recognize in *this* visible spectacle, this visage and shape, these gestures and words, the definitive and incomparable mark that the invisible holiness imposes upon common visibility, the τύπος in and as which God condescends to be made seen as well as seen poorly, allowing itself to be both known [*connaître*] and misunderstood [*méconnaître*]. The type of the Cross—the sign of the Cross—bears the mark where the invisible Holy is given with such little reservation that the immediate rupture of its glory is there abandoned. The irremediable mark of the invisible in the visible thus takes the shape of the Cross.

Why the Cross precisely? Because the τύπος where the invisible holiness demeans itself [*s'abaisse*] should be put together with what the visible offers to it in return: the type so receives the mark of the invisible *ad modum recipientis.* And yet the history of men coincides with the history of murder and of hatred toward God and the innocent; as a result, the visible receives the mark of the invisible in it only according to the mode of its own murderous hatred for the invisible itself—according to the mode of refusal, even to the point of killing it. In this struggle, the invisible remains innocent: it is thus not the invisible that will forcibly brand the visible; it is on the contrary the visible that will mark the invisible with a fatal blow; and even while receiving a mark, it will be only to the second degree: the indelible mark of the blood of the innocent, of the blood of the invisible, marked first by the hatred that the visible has for it. The τύπος of the invisible on the visible will at first exhibit the murderous mark that the visible inflicts upon the invisible that loves it: in short, the wounds of Christ on the Cross. In order to recognize the holiness and innocence of the invisible God, man henceforth has at his disposal a visible mark—the wounds he has inflicted upon the body of God. Thus appears the type of the Cross: not a sacred image imitating the divine and exhibiting in itself a spectacle, but the imprint paradoxically received by the invisible in the manifest wound that the invisible imposes on it. The spear-pierced side of the visible Christ is there made to appear suddenly as the type of the invisible. So also the τύπος τού σταυροῦ [type of the cross] on which the Second Council of Nicaea grounds the icon, if it can be authorized only by a single occurrence of τύπος in the Gospels, is precisely the site of the death on the Cross: "The other disciples [*sc.* Thomas called Didymus] were saying to him, 'We have seen the Lord!' But he said to them: 'Unless I shall see in his hands the mark of the nails (τύπον τών ἥλων), I will not believe" (John 20:25). The mark of the nails could never have been inscribed in the hands—practically the holes of the invisible within the visible flesh—if the holiness of the Holy had not first consented to suffer the mark of its being refused by the hatred of men. The mark of this refusal would not itself become thinkable unless the invisible holiness first made it visible thanks to the exposure of its advance. The icon thus finds its logic and its unique legitimacy only in the repetition—this time between the face of the resurrected Christ ("colors, mosaics, and other suitable materials") and an irreducible approximation (παραπλησίως)—of the paradox of recognition without spectacle which sees the visible tool of torture as the invisible holiness of a Living One, who nevertheless died there. Such a repetition breaks here with every imitation, since the one moves from the visible to the visible by resemblance, whereas the other moves from the visible to the invisible by recognition [*reconnaissance*].

To regard the Cross as a type and not merely as an object of sight it is thus necessary to see (thus recognize and confess) in the marks made upon his body the stigmata of the invisible attested by the sin of humanity; the gallows exhibit only a corpse, which, according to the logic of the mimetic, would resemble nothing—but the Cross, like the sign of the

Cross, offers to the one who will confess, according to the logic of the type, the Son of God. Thus the Cross, when thus sighted, becomes an icon. On this model and by repeating this hermeneutic transition, we can "approximately" specify the icon—admittedly, here, the visible tool of recognition is adorned with various materials ("colors, mosaics, and other suitable materials") and no longer by the wood of the gallows; but the invisible remains in both cases, the holiness of the Holy and the glory of the Son. The common icon thus no more imitates the Cross than the Cross imitates the invisible holiness; the common icon repeats the transition from the visible to the invisible that made the Cross the sign of the glory of the Holy. Just as Thomas recognized his Lord in the very type that offered the trace of the nails, so also the faithful can recognize their Lord in the visible types that are drawn by artists. In both cases, it is not necessary to see the visible as a spectacle, but necessary rather to pick up the trace that there records the tracks of the invisible. So the icon can be contemplated with honor only by a gaze that venerates it as the stigmata of the invisible. Only the one who prays can thus climb from the visible to the invisible (according to the logic of the type), whereas the spectator can only compare the visible to the visible (according to the logic of the mimetic). To the saints these things are holy: only the one who prays crosses the icon, because he alone knows the function of type.

III

The recognition, without imitation, in the τύπος of the One who is marked should not be taken as a mere recording in this imprint itself. The τύπος, even the one of the Cross, draws nothing of the invisible in it, but, by an effect of inverted perspective,[12] does not cease to let itself be drawn by it. The second characteristic of the icon determined by the Second Council of Nicaea follows from this: precisely to recognize and so to confess the holiness of that of which it bears the mark. And yet the holiness does not reside in the icons any more than it lives in the Cross under the mode of being one visible spectacle among others. The type of the icon, like the type of the Cross, owes its holiness, transitively, to Christ; but Christ himself holds his invisible holiness only by virtue of his return, permanent and total, to the invisible Father; it is to the Father that he visibly gives his spirit (παρέδοχεν τὸ πνεῦμα, John 19:30), who alone is holy. By this return he truly accomplishes his title of "holy one of God" (Mark 1:24=John 6:69): Christ testifies to his righteous [*juste*] holiness only by testifying to the unique holiness of the Father; it is by never claiming his own holiness or his own glory, therefore it is only by giving back absolutely to his Father that he takes up that holiness that is given back to him in order to be glorified; Christ attains his holiness by coming undone [*se défaisant*] for the sake of the Father, by making sure that henceforth, all holiness finds its fulfillment in its transfer by itself toward the invisible Holy. The Cross bears the τύπος of holiness only insofar as it exemplifies this transfer. From then on it becomes clear that the common icon can merit any fragment of the glory of the Holy only insofar as it returns all holiness to that One of which it visibly bears the mark, "approximately," just as the Cross bears the mark of Christ's own return of all holiness to One other than himself, the Father. The icon repeats, to a degree largely disseminated, the return of holiness to the Holy One; and this return alone testifies to the holiness of the One that thus casts off holiness. The icon thus displays, in the humility of time and space, the unique act of return which, accomplished on the Cross, revealed economically the original return of the Son to the Father in the Spirit, according to eternal theology. The logic of this return alone qualifies an icon as holy, whether an icon made by human hands, or the Son, the "icon of the invisible God" (Colossians 1:15).[13] Returning—or better, being returned—to the only Holy One, the icon finds its fulfillment in definitively relinquishing any claim to imitate the Holy One to which it returns and which returns in it [*auquel elle se remet et s'en remet*]; if an appropriateness can be ascribed to it, this would be due to unmerited grace and by virtue of a communion of will, never due to the adequacy of any intrinsic correspondence; for the imitation always tries to revert to a model that constitutes an ideal, in order to glorify itself as much as possible; but the icon has nothing that it has not received. It renounces, by an aesthetic asceticism, any mimetic rivalry with glory. Whereas in imitation, the more the derived image is perfected, the less it depends upon the glory of its model, to the point that the tangential autarchy of the glory inevitably drives it to the self-reference of an idol, the icon, on the contrary, glorifies itself only by returning all glory to the invisible. Iconoclasm criticizes the supposed idolatrous derivation of icons, because it persists in interpreting according to the logic of similitude and mimetic rivalry, without ever suspecting—or accepting—that the τύπος has categorically broken away from any imitation of an original. The icon does not represent; it presents—not in the sense of producing a new presence (as in painting) but in the sense of making present the holiness of the Holy One. The icon is ordered to holiness by never claiming it for itself. And, since holiness is indicated in the prayer that it returns to the invisible, one will say with the Second Council of Nicaea, "the more often [Christ, the Virgin, and the saints] are looked upon through their iconic mark (δι᾽εἰκονικῆς ἀνατυπώσεως ὁρῶνται), the more those that contemplate them testify (διανίστανται), in kissing them, a respectful veneration (προσκύνησις), but not a true adoration (λατρεία), which is reserved for the divine nature."[14] The icon admits and calls for veneration, but it is nevertheless exempt from any idolatry, and on two grounds.

First, this veneration is not to be confused with an adoration. Since adoration is reserved exclusively for the divine nature, it is necessary to conclude that the icon does not claim either to represent or above all to constitute the divine nature; this is equivalent to saying, following common patristic distinctions, that it aims only at the person (ὑποστάσι) and face (προσώπον) of Christ.[15] The Incarnation, which delivers the person of Christ and the divine nature, only prolongs the presence of this nature in the Eucharist, where no face accompanies it, and vice versa: it grants legitimacy to the icon, a perpetual visage of Christ waiting for his return, with the sacramental accompaniment of the divine nature. It is precisely this distortion of the economy that prevents the danger of the idol: the Church can never identify the nature and the hypostatic visage of its Christ in a single liturgical performance, nor yield to the ultimate temptation of summoning as a demon that which it should dominate. Hence the importance of not including the common icon under the title of "sacrament." The icon thus strictly retains its paradoxical legitimacy as τύπος: a sign and not (a) nature of the invisible—appearing at a distance from the invisible, precisely because the invisible marks it all the way through.

Consequently, the icon, by refusing to receive adoration for the sake of a simple veneration, thus already accomplishes the same by returning this veneration to the invisibility of the unique Holy One. The icon never ceases to (be) return(ed) to the crucial τύπος of Christ, not only because it is not by nature the Christ, but above all because its very function is to help believers to give back veneration to Christ alone. The icon proclaims itself a useless servant of a veneration that it does not touch, but before which it effaces itself to the point of transparency. The icon is not the idol of Christ precisely because it returns (and is returned) to him: the τύπος uniquely points to its πρωτοτύπων. In order to clarify the importance of the "memory of prototypes (πρωτοτύπων)," the Second Council of Nicaea cites the celebrated formula of Saint Basil: "The honor given to the icon is transferred (διαβαίνει) to the prototype."[16] What prototype deserves to have the icon exile itself in this way? Canon 7 immediately responds: "and he who venerates an icon venerates in it the hypostasis of the One who is there depicted." The icon, by refusing the role of being merely a mimetic image, reaches the person of the other as such; the visible opens not onto another visible but onto the other *of* the visible—the invisible Holy One. The icon does not fight against any original by imitation; it reaches the invisible by never ceasing to transgress itself, according to the paradox of ἀνατυπώσις. In the icon, the gaze walks along itself toward an invisible gaze that envisages it from glory.

IV

The icon steps outside of the mimetic logic of the image by what it accomplishes entirely in its reference to a prototype—an invisible prototype. This definition, however, is open to an immediate objection: Can the invisibility of the prototype guarantee the visibility of the icon? By renouncing the relation of similitude, does not the prototype abandon the icon to a common and unpretentious visibility? From this follows a second objection: If veneration should pass through the visible icon in order to be referred to the invisible of the prototype, would it not be appropriate to dispense with such an ambiguous and certainly misleading intermediary, and instead go directly to the thing itself? The hypothesis of an-iconic veneration of an imperceptible original comes down to, and thus recovers, the temptation of a mimetic relation between two homogeneous spectacles; both oppose the icon with an iconoclastic [*iconomaque*] reaction more powerful still than the one condemned by the Second Council of Nicaea, since it unites the entire history of metaphysics normally held as two extremes: Plato and Nietzsche. What metaphysics opposes to the icon is nothing other than its own aporia before the invisible secret of the visible.

According to the established Platonic position, what we are tempted to understand as an icon has a function only of addition, which later ends up doubling what alone *is*: this ὕστερον γεγονὸς εἴδωλον [need for idols] (*Republic*, II.382c), under the belated activity of the worker (painter, artisan, project manager, etc.), argues with what is (the thing existing outside of its causes); indeed, this production thus redoubles a first redoubling, the one that the existing thing imposes upon what should already be present to the consciousness of the worker/artist: the ideal model—τὸ εἶδος . . . ὅ δή φαμεν εἶναι ὅ ἔστι κλίνη (*Republic*, X.597a), that is to say, the essence and pure form of the thing still to come, which alone is in nature (ἡ ἐν τῇ φύσει οὖσα, ibid., 597b). According to the example chosen by Plato, there are three couches: the ὄντως couch, the only real one, imperceptible [*insensible*] but nevertheless obvious [*evident*]; next, the actual, individual couch; and finally the imitation of the imitation, the image painted by the artist. Here the logic of imitation increases visibility in direct proportion to sensibility, thus in inverse proportion to truth and reality. Access to the original and essential being [*l'étant*] requires canceling out the visible and sensible intermediaries as so many distorting filters (literally: those that deform the form, what we might call "enemies of the *eidos*" ["*eido-maques*"]), whose most elaborate colors mix only to obfuscate the anterior light; thus the invisible reality will reappear only when the brilliant luminosity of things and images fades. When Hegel defines the work of art as a "sign of the idea" ("Signs of the Idea," *Encyclopedia of the Philosophical Sciences*, §556), he once again radicalizes the Platonic decision; basically, art is thus reduced to presenting in the sensibility of intuition (thus in the abstract) what is discovered in and by the self only in the accomplished rationality of the idea (which alone is concrete); art assures a mediated, provisional, and mimetic access to the invisible of pure intelligibility. In the two dominant figures of its dogmatic accomplishment, metaphysics thus admits (to being) iconoclastic [*iconomaque*]: the image imitates the original, which alone *is*; it remains sensible (thus aesthetic) with respect to the original, which alone is intelligible, thus imperceptible and invisible (science and absolute knowledge); the weight of glory must directly relate to the original, by deserting images as mere idols. The original cancels out [*annule*] the image (at least in the end): the invisible, equivalent to only the intelligible, effaces all evidence of itself from every sensible image, just as the light of day blackens a photographic film that is exposed out in the open. Being iconoclastic, metaphysics condemns the image to the rank of an idol.

But we no longer belong to the dogmatic epoch of metaphysics; we inhabit the era of nihilism, where metaphysics draws to a close under the mode of a disappearance. Has not iconoclasm—from Platonism to Hegel—disappeared in the epoch of what Nietzsche defined as the inversion of Platonism and the devaluation of all values? On the contrary, it is necessary to recognize that the idolatrous status of the image has never attained its ultimate consequences more than with Nietzsche. Several arguments can be advanced to establish this point.

First, Nietzsche disputes the notion that an intelligible and imperceptible original precedes and rules the sensible as reducible to the rank of imitation, for the presumed original maintains its purity at the price of negations so complete that it can no longer attest to its reality; neither visible nor actual nor efficacious, it is reduced to a shadow of the reality that it flees by believing it precedes it. But is this "otherworld [*arrière-monde*]" imitated by what he names its image, or, on the contrary, is it not the other that imitates it and, as a result, liberates it as the only actual reality? The unequal relation between the original and the image remains, but it is inverted: the image alone *is*, it alone deserves praise, and it alone accounts for the inexistence of the original. We can point out already that, even inverted, the relation of mimetic rivalry here always remains operative: even more, the same inversion confirms that this rivalry dominates the entire debate concerning the visible and the invisible. Is it, however, necessary to conclude that the image, in being liberated from the yoke of its original, has necessarily escaped the status of an idol?

Second, and on the contrary, Nietzsche radicalizes the idolatrous interpretation of every image. Indeed, if he liberates the image from the original that supposedly devalued it, he subjects it to the person who sees it and evaluates it. The image depends all the more upon a spectator when it is divorced from its original. In Nietzschean terms, one might say: to see a visible involves defining (and producing) a spectacle. This definition ultimately comes down to an evaluation, but every evaluation points, before the evaluated, to an evaluator. Every evaluation is performed by a will to power that attests to and thus recognizes this or that evaluation: "Therefore he calls himself 'man,' which means: the esteemer. To esteem is to create: hear this, you creators! Esteeming itself is of all esteemed things the most estimable pleasure" (*Thus Spake Zarathustra* 1, §14).[17] By taking on the status of a value evaluated by a will to power, the image is liberated from its intelligible original only in order to be subjected to man, the estimator—which henceforth becomes the unique original, thus taking the place of all originals. To put this in more phenomenological terms: the visible that a gaze keeps under its view represents (*vorstellen*) less an original invisible and more of a representing (*vertreten*) in the sensible of the scope of this gaze itself; if this gaze stops at this visible, it is because there it discovers the maximum or optimal extent of spectacle that it can support or desire; this gaze no longer transgresses the visible, because it is precisely there that it recognizes itself. From that point on the image imitates its viewer first and does not open onto any original other than its solitary spectator; the gaze is said to be in the visible "which tells it something." The image becomes the idol of man—"man is the original of his idol" (Feuerbach)[18]—but even more, man is self-idolized in the visible that he chooses himself in a spectacle. Thus the inversion of Platonism does not put an end to metaphysical iconoclasm; it radicalizes it. It is no longer a matter of a provisional, amendable idolatry of images, imitating at a distance the intelligible that itself remains pure; rather, here we have a self-idolatry, where man, as estimator of all values, can or should, as regards the world, live only on images of his obsessed will to power. Man becomes obsessed by only ever being able to see the images modeled on himself; by virtue of seeing without being seen, he can see nothing but the mirror images of his own gaze. The besieged obscenity of a universe of idols does not permit a single exit, since the gaze will always only reproduce its idols. And on the forestage [*l'avant-scène*] that does not overhang any "otherworld," the sacrifice will execute the very one that it means to glorify—man, original invisible of haunting images.

With this self-idolatry—where the image is reduced to its spectator as its only original—not only do we bring out the coherence of the two extremes of metaphysical iconoclasm; we also reach our world in its accomplished state of idolatry. For what one calls, very often without thinking about it, an "audiovisual civilization," thus a "world of images," presupposes precisely this self-idolatry. Indeed, a "world of images" becomes possible only if images can still open onto their supposed contrary, the actuality of an original in which to dwell. How did the "world of images" not go stale in a mere world of paper? Because, of course, the images themselves are henceforth valued as actualities [*effectivités*]. How can the distinction between the image and the actual be thus abolished? Because a new term mediates them: man, who actually creates these visible products (things [*perceptibles*] in general), in which, however, he gives only himself to be seen, under a million different roles and by a million and one different schemes. This equivalence can go from the image to the actual reality: the image produces itself with an ever-increasing technical perfection (well said to be a "hologram"), in a way that gives rise to the most efficacious of actual effects in the souls of men (propaganda, publicity, pornography, etc.). What makes these images effective is their ability to satisfy the imaginary needs of their "targets"; thus, in the end, it is their ability to be conformed, precisely as idols, to the expectation and the supposed scope of their spectators. The same equivalence can go, inversely, from the actuality to the image: perhaps the will to power should not only evaluate but be evaluated, thus pushed forward [*se faire évaluer, donc se faire valoir*]; what comes back is made seen by being transposed as completely as possible into an image; but "to create an image" requires that I first reduce myself to an idol measured exactly to the gaze that I want to capture; "public idols" secure veneration only by exhausting themselves in the public's gaze and desire, thus strictly by idolatry in every case. In both operations, the mediation fully rests on the idolatrous function. But in order for it to be put to work, it is necessary that a gaze want to see itself in the desire, pleasure, or fear of other gazes. It is not a matter there, first of all, of either a prostitution or a thirst for power; or rather, these are themselves already derived from self-idolatry.

Thus the objections addressed by the mimetic logic of the image to the doctrine of the icon do not define a past debate. Some indications have sufficed to establish that they renew themselves in the most contemporary situation of the visible—the disaster of the image. As a result, if the icon can resist metaphysical iconoclasm, it would be necessary to infer that it covertly responds to our current situation.

V

According to mimetic logic, the image doubles in the visible what the original keeps in the invisible. A number of aporias result from the simplicity of this opposition: what "is" is neither seen nor perceived nor given; what is seen, perceived, and given "is" not. If the icon is to escape from such aporias, it could be known only by moving beyond, or at least displacing, what appears to be a clear-cut opposition. The question thus becomes: How do the visible and the invisible organize themselves between the τύπος and the πρωτοτύπος [prototype]? Consider the most trivial occurrence—that of an icon, an object of worship, before it is lost in "a work of art": the visible surface of the wood there gives to be seen, surrounded by a face, two eyes; these two painted eyes, however, permit themselves to be intentionally pierced (thus under a mode that is irreal) by the invisible weight of a gaze; in short, in these two dots of basically black paint, I discern not only the visible image of a gaze that is (like all gazes) invisible but, provided that I acquiesce to it, this gaze in person, which, in fact, envisages me. Through the merely painted icon, I discover myself visible and seen by a gaze that, though present in the sensible, remains invisible to me. How then do the visible and the invisible coincide? We have already indicated the answer: intentionally. But how can intentionality here traverse from the visible to the invisible and from the other to myself, while in strict phenomenology it exerts itself from a visible intended object [*un visible visant*] to a visible aim [*un visible visé*] and in the field of an aim in terms of myself [*à partir de moi*]? Without a doubt because here the aim is inverted: it comes in no way from my gaze, but from an invisible gaze that engenders the visibility of its face and then envisages me as visible. This paradox demands a more complete justification; we borrow it from Christology, following the hypothesis concerning the intentional unity of the visible with the invisible in the icon, as an object of the world, aesthetically repeating what the hypostatic union of natures indeed accomplished in Christ, as a paradigm of the universe. Briefly: the visible humanity gives to be recognized in the person of Christ the invisible divinity; this divinity, however, was not in any way directly visible in the humanity of Christ, just as his gaze is not immediately given as a spectacle on the painted wood of the icon. If Christ constitutes, as εἰκων τοῦ θεοῦ τοῦ ἀοράτου [icon of the invisible] (Colossians 1:15), the paradigm of the aesthetic icon, this is in no way because he dispels the ambiguous commerce between the visible and the invisible; it is, on the contrary, because he fulfills its most extreme danger. In his person, human nature becomes, entirely, the type whose prototype consists of nothing less than the divine nature. Thus the aesthetic relation still limited to a visible spectacle (a painted face) is radicalized to its prototype, type of an invisible counter-intentionality (a gaze in person). The difficulty of recognizing on the painted wood of the icon the invisible gaze of Christ precisely reproduces the absolute difficulty of confessing that on the wood of the Cross the divine nature of the Son of God dies according to his humanity, the mortal sufferings of invisible holiness in the horror of visible sin. But the hypostatic union guarantees the intentional unity only by the strictly divine equivalence that enables Christ to say: "The one who has seen me has seen the Father" (John 14:9). Only the intratrinitarian communion, according to the Holy Spirit, between the Son and the Father, legitimates it, as a permanent transition from an eternal type to an eternal prototype that cannot be circumvented—a transition from the hypostatic transitivity of the natures in Christ (from that point eternal) to the intentional transitivity of the visible and the invisible in the aesthetic icon (henceforth a derivative icon). The Trinitarian basis opens up a definitive and unsurpassable distance, which only the Spirit can cross without respite and yet without movement. And this is moreover why He alone renders possible the confession of Christ and the veneration of the icon. Certainly the aesthetic icon manages a remarkable commerce between the visible and the invisible; certainly, contrary to iconoclastic logic, it does not freeze these two terms in two sites, separated by imitation. But precisely the visible and the invisible should not move from one extreme of the icon to the other (and back), since they do not circulate as such at first even within the hypostatic union of natures. And this is only mobilized and brought under the control of only the perichoric relation of the persons of the Trinity: the ultimate icon is thus revealed as a "living icon of charity," according to the salutary formulation of Maximus the Confessor.[19] From this comes a consequence, in fact the principle of the icon: the icon breaks with the rigid distribution of the visible in the sensible and the invisible in the intelligible, because it substitutes for an imitation that divides them a transition that does not cease to exchange them. This transition does not manage the visible and the invisible but organizes them with a view to revealing what neither one of them can manifest on its own: the charity that provides the impetus for the transition itself, a movement from the Son to the Father before any passage from type to prototype or from visible to invisible. According to this transition, charity reveals that the Father is given in and as the Son, that the prototype is opened in and as the visible. But these kenotic transitions never testify to charity. They can thus appear only for the one who goes back to them, according to the same kenotic transition by which charity is offered in a paradox. The idol culminates in the visible glory that it appropriates for itself; the icon is completed in the paradox of an invisible holiness, from which it is torn. Thus the icon also overcomes the metaphysical iconoclasm of our time.

VI

The resolutions established by the Second Council of Nicaea find their conceptual scope in the contemporary debate. They call into question, in the name of the icon as an "icon of charity," the logic of the idol right up to its last mode, self-idolatry. We can note these oppositions point by point.

First, the icon objects to every reduction of the visibility in it to the rank of a mere spectacle; it is not exhausted in an object opened to the gaze of a spectator who is able to see it for himself. For before being viewed and seen [*être vue et à voir*], the icon silently demands from its visitor that he be seen by it and that, through the visible object, the invisible gaze of the visitor be opened to see the sudden appearance of another invisible gaze. The icon wants its interlocutors to envisage it, face to face, whereas the idol is satisfied with merely satisfying a gaze obsessed with its own spectacle.

Next, the icon liberates the image from the mimetic rivalry between the visible and the invisible, definitively frozen in two extremes: it substitutes the original, or the invisible exhausted in the intelligible, with the prototype. The prototype strikes the image with its mark and testifies to it without similitude, so that in response the mark thus made itself testifies in the movement of its return to the prototype; for similitude (and the rivalry that it provokes), the icon substitutes fidelity (and the intentional communion that it permits). The mark [*marque*], like every sign, does not claim to (be) give(n) to be seen, but intends to be recognized (and recognize itself) as the prototype that marks it. This transition of recognition plays out just as well within the visible (common sign) or the invisible (between the Father and the Son) as at their limit (in the aesthetic icon or in the face of Christ). Rather than being merely an object, the image then becomes the site of a reciprocal transition, thus the instrument of a communion.

Then, letting itself be pierced by another gaze, the icon requires it to render a gaze—the alms of a gaze—which envisages it as it envisages. In order that the gaze thus rendered not become, again, the setting of a pure spectacle (idol), it is necessary that the gaze given by the icon admit a new modality of operation: veneration. For the προσκύνησις [veneration] comes from a gaze that is bent toward the sun and thus neither sees head-on nor is able to object to what it welcomes; this gaze does not see at first, but is exposed to being seen without seeing, thus recognizing in the painted visible the anteriority and real alterity of an other-than-itself. Thus the icon leads us to question the objectification, production, and consummation to which iconoclasm reduces the modern image.

Finally, the icon receives and expects a veneration that, however, it never appropriates for itself. The praise received is immediately transformed in a paradox of glory transmitted and lost; indeed the icon deserves veneration only insofar as it shows an other-than-itself and thus becomes the pure type of the prototype, toward which it does not cease to return absolutely. The image extricates itself from idolatry by constantly destroying the screen of its visibility, in order to become impoverished, as the pure sign of that which marks it; the visible is opened, as an abyss or sky that transpierces the obsession with the world. Our imprisoning "world of images" would not admit a single escape to the least bit of freedom if it weren't for the once and for all piercing of the spear that opened the side of Christ.

The icon thus contradicts point by point the modern determination of the image, following the ruthless demands of metaphysical iconoclasm. Far from managing a new spectacle, it allows it to point to another gaze. Far from comparing the visible to the invisible by a mimetic rivalry, it bears the mark of the blow of a prototype by which it is recognized. Far from prostituting itself in a self-idolatrous spectacle, it solicits a veneration that it does not cease to transmit to its prototype. It thus defines itself as the other gaze of a prototype, which demands the veneration of my own gaze climbing, across this type, toward it. The icon has as its only interest the crossing of gazes—thus, strictly speaking, love. In contrast to dogmatic metaphysics, the icon saves the image from the status of illusion, alienated from an invisible and intelligible original. In contrast to metaphysics in a state of nihilism, the icon saves the image from self-idolatry, thus from the foreclosure of the "world of images." Neither orphan of the invisible nor prisoner of the visible, the image that takes up the role of the icon again becomes the bond of a communion. The image-affirming [*iconodoule*] doctrine of the Second Council of Nicaea concerns not only nor first of all a point in the history of ideas, nor even a decision of Christian dogma: it formulates above all an—perhaps the only—alternative to the contemporary disaster of the image. In the icon, the visible and the invisible embrace each other from a fire that no longer destroys but rather lights up the divine face for humanity.

Bibliographical Note

The texts collected here constitute reworked versions of previous publications.

Chapter 1 was originally published as "La croisée du visible et l'invisible," in *Trois essais sur la perspective,* Editions de la Différance, Paris, 1985.

Chapter 2 takes up and completely transforms the theses first advanced in *Jean-François Lacalmontie: "Ce que cela donne,"* Éditions de la Différence, Paris, 1986.

Chapter 3 reproduces "L'Aveugle à Siloé (ou le report de l'image à son original)," which appeared in *Revue catholique internationale: Communio,* XII, 6, Paris, November 1987.

Chapter 4 draws on "Le prototype de l'image," a presentation given to the international colloquium on the Second Council of Nicaea, held at the Collège de France, October 2–4, 1986. The proceedings of this colloquium were edited by F. Boespflug and N. Losskey, and published under the title *Nicée II, 787–1987: Douze siècles d'images religieuses,* Paris, Les éditions du Cerf, 1987.

I would like to thank R. Brague, the editor of *Revue catholique internationale: Communio,* and N.-J. Sed, the literary editor at Editions due Cerf, for permission to utilize these sources.

Translator's Note

In order to preserve the centrality of the author's voice, translator's notes have been added only to refer to English sources, to explain select translation decisions, to indicate a parallel discussion in other works by Jean-Luc Marion as a way of explaining a particular interpretation behind the translation, or to provide explanations for readers in aesthetics who might not be acquainted with the terminology of phenomenology that informs Marion's work.

The completion of this project has put me in the debt of many. I would like to thank Tom Carlson for first opening the door that gave me the opportunity to work on this translation, and Jeff Kosky for setting the standard for any translator of Marion's work. Thanks also to Helen Tartar, of Stanford University Press, for her encouragement and patience, and to Nancy Young for her careful copyediting, which much improved the book. Darren Dahl generously agreed to read a draft of the manuscript, providing both support and helpful criticism, and Otto Selles, my colleague in French, provided strategic assistance in the eleventh hour. Jean-Luc Marion kindly answered my queries with grace. I am grateful for his provocative work in phenomenology and am happy to acknowledge my debt to his thought.

My wife, Deanna, prodded me in my labors and kept me accountable, for which I am grateful. And finally, *grâce à Dieu* for graciously granting me, as it were, the gift of tongues.

Notes

1. THE CROSSING OF THE VISIBLE AND THE INVISIBLE

1. Marion refers here to technical considerations of "perspective" in art. It is closely linked with concerns about "the gaze" or "view" in phenomenology. At stake here in particular, as Marion will indicate, is a whole theory of "constitution."—Trans.

2. While *spectacle* generally refers to a "sight" (as in "a sight to behold"), I have for the most part translated the French word with the English "spectacle," to indicate a technical interest in the object of sight.—Trans.

3. René Char, "L'Absent," in *Fureur et Mystère*, p. 39, or *Oeuvres complètes*, La Pléiade Series (Paris, 1983), p. 140.

4. Cyril of Alexandria, *Le Christ est un*, in *Patrologiae Cursus, series Graecae*, ed. Migne (cited hereafter as *PG*), vol. 75, 753c; or in G. M. de Durand, ed., *Deux dialogues christologiques*, Sources chrétiennes series, vol. 97 (Paris, 1964), pp. 430–32.

5. Following Thomas A. Carlson's practice in his translation of Jean-Luc Marion's *God Without Being* (Chicago, 1991), I have sometimes rendered *la vue* as "the gaze," which usually translates *le regard*.—Trans.

6. At stake here is the theme of "saturation," of a donation that gives itself in excess—*contra* the themes of adequation and fulfillment in Husserl. Thus, this discussion should be considered in light of Marion's notion of the "saturated phenomenon."—Trans.

7. The French term *vide* presents special problems in this chapter, possessing a range of meaning that includes "vacuum," "space," and "void." I have sometimes used different words to translate *vide* but have generally indicated the French word in brackets.—Trans.

8. This is a term employed in Husserl's phenomenology.—Trans.

9. Friedrich Nietzsche, *Wille zur Macht*, §567, or Colli-Montinari 14 [184] (*Nietzsche Werke*, vol. 8, 3 [Berlin, 1962], p. 163). [The English translation is from Friedrich Nietzsche, *The Will to Power*, trans. Walter Kaufmann and R. J. Hollingdale (New York, 1967), p. 305.]

10. In contemporary French philosophers such as Derrida and Marion, *relève* is used to translate *Aufhebung* (Hegel). (See especially Jean-Luc Marion, "Metaphysics and Phenomenology: A Relief for Theology," *Critical Inquiry* 20 [1994]: 572–91.) Here the play is on a "lifting up" that creates a "relief," in the sense of a work of art that includes a texture of depth, or as in a "relief map," which indicates depth.—Trans.

11. On this painting, see the excellent commentary by D. Coutagne, "Le Miroir d'un mariage. Le réalisme religieux dans 'Les époux Arnolfinit' de Jean Van Eyck," *Communio* 4, no. 5 (Sept. 1979).

12. Marcel Proust, *A la recherche du temps perdu*, La Pléiade Series, vol. 1, p. 840.

13. Or an "empty emptiness," referring to the double emptiness of perspective.—Trans.

14. I have translated *irréelle* as "irreal," rather than simply "unreal," because "irreal" is an important term in Husserl's phenomenology, which functions as the backdrop for Marion's discourse.—Trans.

15. Paul Cézanne, *Conversations avec Cézanne*, ed. P. M. Doran (Paris, 1978), p. 132.

16. "Bedazzlement" is the mode of "disappearance" that attends the saturated phenomenon.—Trans.

17. C. Malévitch, *De Cézanne au suprématisme*, in *Premier tome des écrits*, trans. Fr. J.-C. and V. Marcadé (Lausanne, 1974), p. 102.

18. In English in the original.—Trans.

19. We follow here, particularly on the difference between Pollock and Hantaï, the conclusions of Y. Michaud, "Métaphysique de Hantaï," in the catalogue *Simon Hantaï*, Biennale de Venise 1982 (Paris, 1980).

20. C. Malévitch, *Du cubisme et du futurisme au suprématisme*, in *Premier tome des écrits*, pp. 65–66. The first two versions of this text expressly underline that "the futurists, while forbidding the painting of feminine thighs, the copying of portraits, have also removed perspective" (p. 38).

21. See, for example, Malévitch, *Premier tome des écrits*, pp. 60–61ff. This point and several others receive a firm interpretation in the dense but decisive study by E. Martineau, *Malévitch et la philosophie* (Lausanne, 1977).

22. C. Malévitch, *Le Suprématisme*, trans. A. Robel-Chicurel, in C. Malévitch, *Écrits*, ed. A. B. Nakov (Paris, 1975), p. 213.

23. Malévitch, *Du cubisme et du futurisme*, p. 67.

24. C. Malévitch, *Introduction à la théorie de l'élément ajouté en peinture*, in Malévitch, *Écrits*, pp. 371 and 379.

25. In early Christian art, an *orant* is a person who is represented in prayer. Thus *l'orant* refers to "the one represented in prayer."—Trans.

26. See Jean-Luc Marion, *Prolégomènes à la charité*, 2d ed. (Paris, 1991), esp.

pp. 107ff. [Jean-Luc Marion, *Prolegomena to Charity*, trans. Stephen Lewis (Bronx, N.Y.: Fordham University Press, 2002), pp. 72ff.].

27. Cited by K. Gallwitz, *Picasso Laureatus: Son oeuvre depuis 1945*, trans. E. Servan-Schreiber (Lausanne and Paris, 1971), p. 95.

2. WHAT GIVES

1. See the admirable and gloomy catalogue *L'Art conceptuel, une perspective*, Exposition du Musée d'Art Moderne de la Ville de Paris, Nov. 22, 1989–Feb. 19, 1990 (Paris, 1989).

2. The language of violation in this context carries the connotation of rape.—Trans.

3. On *ne remonte pas*: *remonter* is very similar in meaning to *relever*, an important term in Marion's thought. In the sentences that follow, Marion plays first on a couplet of *remonte/monte*, then on one of *remontre/montre*.—Trans.

4. Marion's use of the term *miraculé* here and below (section IV) is difficult to translate. The word refers not to a miracle per se, nor merely to the miraculous, but to the one in whom or upon whom a miracle, such as healing, has been performed. In line with Marion's notion of "liberation," I will refer to the *miraculé* of painting as "the one miraculously saved from the unseen."—Trans.

5. Marion's use of the terms *visable* and *invisable* creates a special challenge for English translation. We must first keep in mind the phenomenological discussion of *intentio* behind discussions of *viser*; in other words, at stake here is a notion of intentionality as a mode of intending or aiming at an object. Stephen Lewis translates *invisable* as "untargetable"; see Jean-Luc Marion, *Prolegomena to Charity*, trans. Stephen Lewis (Bronx, N.Y.: Fordham University Press, 2002), p. 81 n. 8). Kosky, in translating *Étant donné*, leaves the term untranslated; see Jean-Luc Marion, *Being Given*, trans. Jeffrey L. Kosky (Stanford, Calif.: Stanford University Press, 2002), p. 363 n. 41. In translating *Dieu sans l'être*, Carlson usually renders it as "that which cannot be aimed at"; see Jean-Luc Marion, *God Without Being*, trans. Thomas A. Carlson (Chicago, 1991). In this section, I have sometimes translated *visable* as "aimed-at" and *invisable* as "what cannot be aimed at," but at times I have followed Kosky's practice and left it untranslated.—Trans.

6. Marion richly plays here on the Prologue to John's Gospel, where John notes that the Word "came to his own, but his own did not receive him. But as many as received him, to them he gave the right to become children of God" (John 1:11–12). This kenotic movement is analyzed in more detail in Chapter 3 below.—Trans.

7. In English in the original.—Trans.

8. See above, Chapter 1, Section IV.

9. See above, Chapter 1, Section V.

10. We take up here a concept for which we are indebted to the work of Jean-François Lacalmontie, who pointed us to it on the occasion of the essay that we devoted to him under the title *Ce que cela donne* (Paris, 1986). By enlarging here the results of this first approach to the unseen, we do nothing more than generalize what his absolutely exemplary painting has made visible. This return constitutes therefore an homage all the more grateful to his labors. [An "ectype" stands to an archetype as an image stands to a prototype.—Trans.]

11. Here and in what follows, Marion's play on *fond / fonds* presents a challenge. *Fond* can refer to the background of a painting or the bottom of a bag, etc.; *fonds* refers to property, to what one owns. I have usually rendered the latter as "fund," to indicate the "stores" from which something is drawn. In several places, Marion uses the phrase *fond du fonds*, which can be roughly translated as "the core or heart of what one owns." In some places I continue to give the French in brackets in order to signal the play.—Trans.

12. The fragment reads: "The god whose oracle is in Delphi neither speaks out nor conceals, but gives a sign."—Trans.

13. Paul Cézanne, *Conversation avec Cézanne*, ed. P. M. Doran (Paris, 1978), p. 113.

14. I follow here Kosky's practice of leaving this term untranslated (see Marion, *Being Given*, p. 363 n. 41).—Trans.

15. "Ce que cela donne" is the title of this chapter.—Trans.

16. The French *donation* is also used by Marion to translate Husserl's use of the German *Gegebenheit* ("givenness"). However, since the context here is not immediately phenomenological, I have chosen to render it simply as "donation."—Trans.

17. This very difficult phrase could also be rendered as "what gives what gives itself."—Trans.

3. THE BLIND AT SHILOH

1. Marion is playing here on the themes of "credit," "trust," and "faith" as they are linked to monetary discourse: "paper money" is *la monnaie fiduciaire*, and it *accroît* (accrues) its authority from *croire*, "to believe."—Trans.

2. I have left the French *forclusion* untranslated; it is a juridical term that indicates a failure to make one's claim within the statutory time-limit.—Trans.

3. Here Marion plays on the notion of "screen" as it is used in his *God Without Being*—as a *condition* or *medium* through which something is forced to pass, as through a kind of filter.—Trans.

4. Marion refers here to the Church Fathers—for instance, Augustine's critique of *curiositas* as the "lust of the eyes" in *Confessions,* Book X.—Trans.

5. In English in the original, with echoes of Sartre.—Trans.

6. This analysis has already been developed at greater length in my *Prolégomènes à la charité,* 2d ed. (Paris, 1991), pp. 107ff. [Jean-Luc Marion, *Prolegomena to Charity,* trans. Stephen Lewis (Bronx, N.Y.: Fordham University Press, 2002), pp. 72ff.]

7. Most English translations here render *eikon* as "image."—Trans.

8. On the icon, see Jean-Luc Marion, *Dieu sans l'être,* 2d ed. (Paris, 1991), chap. 1 [Jean-Luc Marion, *God Without Being,* trans. Thomas A. Carlson (Chicago, 1991), chap. 1]. On the idol, see my "Ce que nous montre l'idole," in *Rencontres de l'École du Louvre, L'idole* (Paris, 1990), pp. 23–34.

9. The celebrated formula of Irenaeus—"Invisibile etenim Filius, Pater—visibile autem Patris, Filius [The Father is the invisible of the Son, but the Son the visible of the Father]" (*Against Heresies* IV.6.6)—especially must be understood not according to a real partition (the visible part of the Father would be the Son; the invisible part would be the Father) but in terms of an economic manifestation. In other words, "Omnibus igitur revelavit se Pater, ominbus Verbum suum visibilem faciens [The Father has revealed himself to all, by making His Word visible to all]" (ibid., IV.6.5): the Father reveals himself by giving the Son, himself previously invisible. Or again: "Filius revelat agnitionem Patris per suam manifestationem; agnitio enim Patris est Filii manifestatio [The Son reveals the knowledge of the Father through His own manifestation; for the manifestation of the Son is the knowledge of the Father]" (ibid., IV.6.3). Recognizing the invisible Father amounts to accepting the manifestation of the Son. Nothing remains to be shown of paternal invisibility once the Son has shown up in the visible.

10. Marion translates this as *leur marque iconique,* "their iconic mark."

11. Second Council of Nicaea [787], Actio VII, in Mansi, XIII, 378 s; also quoted in R. Denzinger, ed., *Enchiridion Symbolorum,* n. 302, after H. Bettenson, ed., *Documents of the Christian Church,* 2d ed. (Oxford, 1963), p. 94.

12. Saint Basil, *De Spiritu Sancto,* XVIII.45, in *PG,* vol. 32, 149.

13. I have translated this as "shed" rather than "lose," since Marion seems to want to indicate volition on the part of the suffering servant, who *gives up* this glory (cf. Philippians 2:5–11).—Trans.

14. Literally, "impoverished art." This was also the name for an Italian movement in the late 1960s.—Trans.

15. This discussion of objects "duplicated without innovation," and en masse ("to infinity"), foreshadows the discussion (two paragraphs down) of *l'art Saint-Sulpice*—an "art" maligned for its mass production.—Trans.

16. One should sense echoes here of the self-impoverishment of Christ (earlier in this chapter functioning as the paradigm of kenosis, which is itself the paradigm of the image): "For you know the grace of our Lord Jesus Christ, that though he was rich, yet for your sake he became poor [*s'est fait pauvre*], in order that through his poverty you might become rich" (2 Corinthians 8:9).—Trans.

17. While this can also be translated as "ugliness" or "unattractiveness," in accord with the author's theme of impoverishment, I have rendered it as "meanness."—Trans.

18. The descriptive term *sulpicien* derives from a unique Parisian context: in the nineteenth century, a number of shops selling mass-produced religious artifacts (cards, statues, etc.) developed in the area surrounding Saint-Sulpice church in Paris. We might understand these "works of art" as akin to contemporary religious "merchandise," which is mass-produced for the devotion of the faithful but considered by others, from an artistic perspective, to be representative of poor taste, or what we might describe as "kitsch." Marion is here obliquely affirming the function of such art as an example of images that negate themselves and refer the observer to the prototype. Because we have no equivalent term in English (except, perhaps, "Barclay Street art," referring to a comparable market in Manhattan in the nineteenth century), I have opted simply to anglicize the term.—Trans.

19. The Chapelle Matisse, or Chapelle du Rosaire du Dominicaines du Vence, was designed and decorated by Henri Matisse between 1947 and 1951; Jean Cocteau completed the decoration of Chapelle Saint-Pierre (in Villefranche-sur-Mer) in 1957.—Trans.

20. The word also carries the connotation of "overlooking"; thus such a forgetting might be understood as an "oversight."—Trans.

21. Translated above as "mean," and here referring back to Sulpician art.—Trans.

22. Marion's play here is difficult to translate; it could also be translated as "letting myself be seen by the other('s) gaze," that is, be seen by another gaze and by the Other who is gazing.—Trans.

23. Marion here alludes to the story of Jesus' healing of a man blind from birth by spitting on the ground, applying the mud to his eyes, and commanding him to wash himself in the pool of Shiloh or Siloam, which is also called "Sent" (John 9:1–7).—Trans.

4. THE PROTOTYPE AND THE IMAGE

1. The qualifier *iconomaque* literally means "enemy of the icon"; below it will stand in contrast to *iconodoule*, meaning "servant of the icon." To avoid

cumbersome locutions, I have generally translated the former simply as "iconoclastic."—Trans.

2. Given the intentionally phenomenological employment of the term in this context, here I follow Thomas A. Carlson's rendering of *donation* (following Jean-Luc Marion's wishes) as "givenness," in order to indicate its link with *Gegebenheit* in the Husserlian corpus.—Trans.

3. Second Council of Nicaea, Actio VII, after Mansi XIII.378 s; also quoted in R. Denzinger, ed., *Enchiridion Symbolorum*, n. 302. [Marion essentially follows the translation given by C. Von Schönborn, *L'Icône du Christ* (Fribourg: 1976), p. 143. Square brackets are the author's.—Trans.]

4. Marion regularly refers to this passage as "Canon 7" of the Second Council of Nicaea. However, the passage is located in Actio VII, and the canons are distinguished from the actios. When a direct citation is made, I correct the reference to "Actio"; otherwise, I have retained the author's use of "canon."—Trans.

5. Denzinger, *Enchiridion Symbolorum*, nn. 302 and 304, which one should supplement with the Latin version (of Anastase) of the Council of Constantinople IV (869), Canon 3: "typus pretiosae crucis" (ibid., n. 337). See previously Justin, *First Apology*, 60.3.

6. Denzinger, *Enchiridion Symbolorum*, n. 392, citing Saint Basil, *De Spiritu Sancto*, XVIII.45. With this formula, it should be not a matter of a particular theological opinion, but a matter of the fundamental matrix of all doctrine in the service of the icon [*iconodoule*], before and after Nicaea II.

7. John of Damascus, *The Orthodox Faith* [cited hereafter as *Or.*], IV.16, in *PG*, vol. 94, 1169a. Compare the similar formula: "the type and the icon of what was to come" (John of Damascus, *Against Those Who Refuse Icons*, *Or.*, III.26, in *PG*, vol. 94, 1345b).

8. John of Damascus, *Against Those Who Refuse Icons*, *Or.*, 10 and III.21, in *PG*, vol. 94, 1241a and 1341a.

9. John of Damascus, *The Orthodox Faith*, IV.16, in *PG*, vol. 94, 1172b. Note also the fine invective: "While you venerate the icon of the Cross, made from some material, you should not also venerate the icon of the Crucified and of that which bears the salvific cross!" (*Or.*, II.19, in *PG*, vol. 94, 130b).

10. *Or.*, II.11, in *PG*, vol. 94, 1296c (see also *Or.*, III.10, in *PG*, vol. 94, 1033a).

11. The episode in Matthew 13:53–58 indicates not only the distance between the knowledge [*la connaissance*] of Christ (according to the flesh) and the recognition [*reconnaissance*] of him (according to the Spirit), but above all that the invisible absolutely crosses the visible itself. In this sense the blinding of the disciples on the road to Emmaus (Luke 24:17, 25) depicts the hermeneutic situation of every unbelieving gaze before the icon. [For a further exploration of this, see Marion's more recent article "They Recognized Him, and He Became Invisible

to Them," *Modern Theology* 18 (2002): 149ff.—Trans.] It would remain, evidently, to specify the difference between the misunderstanding [*la méconnaissance*] of the Eucharist (substantial presence) and that of the icon (intentional presence).

12. "One can rightly observe, for example, the effectiveness of inverted perspective in the alcove of Daphnée, where the Transfiguration is reproduced; it appears to push us toward our own encounter with the Christ of Glory, between the adoration of Moses and Elijah." L. Bouyer, *Vérité des icons: La tradition iconographique chrétienne et sa signification*, 2d ed. (Paris, 1990), p. 34.

13. The specification of Christ as the icon of the invisible God is directly admitted as being foundational to every doctrine that serves the icon [*iconodoule*]; for example, according to John of Damascus: "The first icon—according to nature and without any parallel—of the invisible God is the Son of the Father" (*Or.*, III.18, in *PG*, vol. 94, 1340a). From this perfect equivalence of form between the Father and the Son (see Saint Basil, *De Spiritu Sancto*, XVIII.45), it then becomes lawful to bring out, according to an increasingly typical parallel, other genres of icons: "those by which God is served" (by which is meant specifically "the wood of the cross" and "the nails"); the Gospels and cultural instruments; icons in the normal sense; and finally our next one, the civil authorities and private authorities. Thus, under the title of "living icon of the invisible God" (John of Damascus, *Or.*, II.15, in *PG*, vol. 94, 1301), of a "living icon, better a living being in itself [ἤντοοῦσα ξωὴ]" (Saint Basil, *Contra Eunome*, I.18, in *PG*, vol. 29, 552b), or of "physical icons" (Theodore Studite, *Antirrheticus*, in *PG*, vol. 99, 501a), Christ determines the rules of every icon and its conditions of validity. The only imitation that can be claimed by the common icon would thus be, contrary to any mimetic aesthetic, the *imitatio Christi*, such that it first rules the life of every believer.

14. Denzinger, *Enchiridion Symbolorum*, n. 302.

15. See, for example, Theodore Studite: "The prototype is in the icon not according to the modality of substance . . . but according to the resemblance of the hypostasis" (*Antirrheticus*, III.3, in *PG*, vol. 99, 420a). Or: "these are two different things, the icon and the prototype, and the difference does not reside in the hypostasis, but is made according to the definition of the substance" (Epistle 212, in *PG*, vol. 99, 1640a). It is necessary to underline that "the image is purely relational" and that its "presence is intentional, pneumatic" (Schönborn, *L'Icône du Christ*, pp. 209 and 224). Just as the hypostasis is concretized in the face (πρόσωπον) and the face itself is made to share the two natures by the union of the two wills, the icon, as long as it is a type of the face, should be contemplated according to the union of wills: the one in prayer [*l'orant*] unites his will to theirs, uni-

fied by Christ in repeating the union of the human will and the divine will by Christ.

16. Saint Basil, *De Spiritu Sancto,* XVIII.45, which depends upon *Letter* XXXVIII.8 (pseudo-Basil? Gregory of Nyssa?), in *PG,* vol. 32, 240a–c, and, among others, Athanasius, *Against the Arians,* III.5, in *PG,* vol. 26, 332a–b.

17. Friedrich Nietzsche, *Thus Spoke Zarathustra,* in *The Portable Nietzsche,* trans. Walter Kaufmann (New York, 1968), p. 171.—Trans.

18. Ludwig A. Feuerbach, *The Essence of Christianity,* trans. George Eliot (New York, 1957). [The original is in Feuerbach, *Gesammelte Werke,* standard ed., (Berlin, 1968), vol. 5, p. 11].

19. "ἀγάπης εἰκόνα," Maximus the Confessor, *Letter* XLIV, in *PG,* vol. 91, 644b. If the Incarnation offers an icon of charity, it would also be necessary conversely to conclude that Christ, by being made charity for men, is given as an icon only by accomplishing charity. Thus charity alone would render the icon possible.

Cultural Memory | in the Present

Jean-Luc Marion, *The Crossing of the Visible*

Eric Michaud, *An Art for Eternity: The Cult of Art in Nazi Germany*

Anne Freadman, *The Machinery of Talk: Charles Peirce and the Sign Hypothesis*

Stanley Cavell, *Emerson's Transcendental Etudes*

Stuart McLean, *The Event and its Terrors: Ireland, Famine, Modernity*

Beate Rössler, ed., *Privacies: Philosophical Evaluations*

Bernard Faure, *Double Exposure: Cutting Across Buddhist and Western Discourses*

Alessia Ricciardi, *The Ends Of Mourning: Psychoanalysis, Literature, Film*

Alain Badiou, *Saint Paul: The Foundation of Universalism*

Gil Anidjar, *The Jew, The Arab: A History of the Enemy*

Jonathan Culler and Kevin Lamb, eds., *Just Being Difficult? Academic Writing in the Public Arena*

Jean-Luc Nancy, *A Finite Thinking*, edited by Simon Sparks

Theodor W. Adorno, *Can One Live after Auschwitz? A Philosophical Reader*, edited by Rolf Tiedemann

Patricia Pisters, *The Matrix of Visual Culture: Working with Deleuze in Film Theory*

Talal Asad, *Formations of the Secular: Christianity, Islam, Modernity*

Dorothea von Mücke, *The Rise of the Fantastic Tale*

Marc Redfield, *The Politics of Aesthetics: Nationalism, Gender, Romanticism*

Emmanuel Levinas, *On Escape*

Dan Zahavi, *Husserl's Phenomenology*

Rodolphe Gasché, *The Idea of Form: Rethinking Kant's Aesthetics*

Michael Naas, *Taking on the Tradition: Jacques Derrida and the Legacies of Deconstruction*

Herlinde Pauer-Studer, ed., *Constructions of Practical Reason: Interviews on Moral and Political Philosophy*

Jean-Luc Marion, *Being Given: Toward a Phenomenology of Givenness*

Theodor W. Adorno and Max Horkheimer, *Dialectic of Enlightenment*

Ian Balfour, *The Rhetoric of Romantic Prophecy*

Martin Stokhof, *World and Life as One: Ethics and Ontology in Wittgenstein's Early Thought*

Gianni Vattimo, *Nietzsche: An Introduction*

Jacques Derrida, *Negotiations: Interventions and Interviews, 1971–1998*, ed. Elizabeth Rottenberg

Brett Levinson, *The Ends of Literature: Post-transition and Neoliberalism in the Wake of the "Boom"*

Timothy J. Reiss, *Against Autonomy: Global Dialectics of Cultural Exchange*

Hent de Vries and Samuel Weber, eds., *Religion and Media*

Niklas Luhmann, *Theories of Distinction: Redescribing the Descriptions of Modernity*, ed. and introd. William Rasch

Johannes Fabian, *Anthropology with an Attitude: Critical Essays*

Michel Henry, *I Am the Truth: Toward a Philosophy of Christianity*

Gil Anidjar, *"Our Place in Al-Andalus": Kabbalah, Philosophy, Literature in Arab-Jewish Letters*

Hélène Cixous and Jacques Derrida, *Veils*

F. R. Ankersmit, *Historical Representation*

F. R. Ankersmit, *Political Representation*

Elissa Marder, *Dead Time: Temporal Disorders in the Wake of Modernity (Baudelaire and Flaubert)*

Reinhart Koselleck, *The Practice of Conceptual History: Timing History, Spacing Concepts*

Niklas Luhmann, *The Reality of the Mass Media*

Hubert Damisch, *A Childhood Memory by Piero della Francesca*

Hubert Damisch, *A Theory of /Cloud/: Toward a History of Painting*

Jean-Luc Nancy, *The Speculative Remark (One of Hegel's Bons Mots)*

Jean-François Lyotard, *Soundproof Room: Malraux's Anti-Aesthetics*

Jan Patočka, *Plato and Europe*

Hubert Damisch, *Skyline: The Narcissistic City*

Isabel Hoving, *In Praise of New Travelers: Reading Caribbean Migrant Women Writers*

Richard Rand, ed., *Futures: Of Derrida*

William Rasch, *Niklas Luhmann's Modernity: The Paradox of System Differentiation*

Jacques Derrida and Anne Dufourmantelle, *Of Hospitality*

Jean-François Lyotard, *The Confession of Augustine*

Kaja Silverman, *World Spectators*

Samuel Weber, *Institution and Interpretation: Expanded Edition*

Jeffrey S. Librett, *The Rhetoric of Cultural Dialogue: Jews and Germans in the Epoch of Emancipation*

Ulrich Baer, *Remnants of Song: Trauma and the Experience of Modernity in Charles Baudelaire and Paul Celan*

Samuel C. Wheeler III, *Deconstruction as Analytic Philosophy*

David S. Ferris, *Silent Urns: Romanticism, Hellenism, Modernity*

Rodolphe Gasché, *Of Minimal Things: Studies on the Notion of Relation*

Sarah Winter, *Freud and the Institution of Psychoanalytic Knowledge*

Samuel Weber, *The Legend of Freud: Expanded Edition*

Aris Fioretos, ed., *The Solid Letter: Readings of Friedrich Hölderlin*

J. Hillis Miller / Manuel Asensi, *Black Holes / J. Hillis Miller; or, Boustrophedonic Reading*

Miryam Sas, *Fault Lines: Cultural Memory and Japanese Surrealism*

Peter Schwenger, *Fantasm and Fiction: On Textual Envisioning*

Didier Maleuvre, *Museum Memories: History, Technology, Art*

Jacques Derrida, *Monolingualism of the Other; or, The Prosthesis of Origin*

Andrew Baruch Wachtel, *Making a Nation, Breaking a Nation: Literature and Cultural Politics in Yugoslavia*

Niklas Luhmann, *Love as Passion: The Codification of Intimacy*

Mieke Bal, ed., *The Practice of Cultural Analysis: Exposing Interdisciplinary Interpretation*

Jacques Derrida and Gianni Vattimo, eds., *Religion*

The authorized representative in the EU for product safety and compliance is:
Mare Nostrum Group
B.V Doelen 72
4831 GR Breda
The Netherlands

www.ingramcontent.com/pod-product-compliance
Lightning Source LLC
LaVergne TN
LVHW051011080826
845145LV00009B/2572

* 9 7 8 0 8 0 4 7 3 3 9 2 2 *